The MASTER'S *Plan*
A Strategy for Making Disciples

Craig Wesley Rench

BEACON HILL PRESS
OF KANSAS CITY

ISBN 978-0-8341-2791-3

Printed in the
United States of America

Cover Design: Doug Bennett
Internal Design: Sharon Page

Library of Congress Cataloging-in-Publication Data

Rench, Craig Wesley.
    The Master's plan : a strategy for making disciples / Craig Wesley Rench.
        p. cm.
    Includes bibliographical references (p.   ).
    ISBN 978-0-8341-2791-3 (pbk.)
    1. Discipling (Christianity) 2. Spiritual formation. 3. Evangelistic work. 4. Witness bearing (Christianity) I. Title.
    BV4520.R46 2011
    268'.8799—dc23

                                                    2011024822

10 9 8 7 6 5 4 3 2 1

This book is lovingly dedicated to my best friend and lover for over forty-three years—my wife, Connie. She has been a constant source of encouragement and blessing to me throughout our years of life and ministry together.
She lives out the principles and priorities of the Master's Plan.
She brings great joy to whoever meets her.
This anointed woman is making disciples of Jesus Christ who in turn make disciples. I am incredibly proud of her and I give God great glory and thanksgiving for this powerful princess of the King of Kings!

Contents

Foreword

I have often used the following quote from Mike Henderson, a passionate discipleship guru: "Jesus said, 'I will build my church.' Our Lord's parting words were, 'You make disciples.' The tragedy is that many of us are trying to build the church while few of us are intentionally making disciples."

The Master's Plan is a holistic approach being used by many Nazarene congregations that emphasizes prayer, evangelism, consolidation, Encounters, open-cell classes, and closed-cell spiritual bands.

Pastor Craig Wesley Rench has written this exceptional book to show us the path toward healthy New Testament church growth. It is based on his research of the Cali, Colombia House of Prayer Church of the Nazarene as well as other congregations that have embraced this model of church life. This research is also a natural extension of his life-long experience as a very effective pastor who makes disciples who make disciples.

Twenty-five years ago I visited the Cali church, pastored by Rev. Adalberto Herrera, and spoke to a congregation of approximately twenty-five persons. In 2011 they averaged over fourteen thousand in worship attendance each week. When you ask Pastor Adalberto and his wife, Nineye, how this growth occurred, they both insist that the turning point was when the church began to pray. This church marches forward on its knees! Over four thousand attend the Wednesday prayer and fasting believer's service. Their worship services, rally services, and open-cell classes are evangelistic, with hundreds and even thousands of persons embracing saving grace in Christ each week. Each new believer receives a phone call and a visit during the week after their conversion. This church is very intentional in bearing "fruit that will remain."

The new believers are grafted into open-cell classes and encouraged to attend a two-day spiritual Encounter weekend. The outcome of this divine grace immersion is a time of radical surrender to God. This is a Pentecost experience in the life of these followers of Christ. The Encounter cluster (twenty to forty believers) then meets weekly for one year for Level One Bible study and leadership development. At the end of that year, each one is challenged to launch an open-cell class. Part of the genius of this approach is that we are not asking cells to produce cells, but rather we are producing leaders who, among other things, start a cell group. They cannot go on to Level Two training until they start a group!

In addition to prayer, evangelism, consolidation, Encounters, and open-cell classes, the pastor begins to prayerfully select persons to join his or her discipleship band. When selecting believers to join a closed-cell band, we should invite the most mature and faithful disciples who have given evidence of their commitment and fruitfulness. In the Cali church, Adalberto has twelve men, Nineye has twelve women, and the youth pastor has twelve students in their discipleship bands. Each of those twelve has twelve.

When the Master's Plan is fully implemented, everyone should be able to answer three questions: "Who is discipling you?" "Who are you discipling?" and "Who are your disciples discipling?"

Programs do not make disciples . . . disciples make disciples.

Some people reject new methods. They refuse to chase the latest fad. The Master's Plan, however, is based on some of the principles the New Testament church employed. These methods were rediscovered in the great Wesley British Isles revival. John Wesley insisted that believers should participate in society meetings (worship services), open classes, and spiritual bands. A colleague general superintendent reported that at a recent assembly, the only churches that were growing were those attempting to implement the Master's Plan.

I invite you to prayerfully read this road map that will guide you and the group you lead to "make Christlike disciples that make Christlike disciples." That was our Master's Plan!

Jerry D. Porter, General Superintendent
International Church of the Nazarene

 one

The Vision of the Father

✦ God Almighty has a vision for your life. He has a plan for your ministry. His design for you is so much grander than anything you could ever fantasize. You have been in the heart and mind of God since eternity past. What he has in store for you goes infinitely beyond your greatest ambitions, hopes, and aspirations. You are important to God. You are vital to the fulfilling of his ultimate vision for the world. By reading this book you've begun fulfilling God's thrilling destiny for your life.

This plan involves you partnering with God in the fulfillment of the Great Commission, Matthew 28:18-20. We are called to multiply spiritual sons and daughters who will, in turn, make more disciples for Jesus. There is no greater cause that we can devote our lives to than helping our Father save his lost children from the devil's eternal lake of fire. Your life will not only impact but change eternity for countless souls.

Discovering God's vision is one of the most important things we will ever do. By committing our lives to God's vision, we will take part in the salvation of countless people. We will be eternally blessed. We will give God great glory by bearing much fruit for him. By pursuing God's vision, we'll also encounter our greatest joy and personal fulfillment.

Nothing else you will ever do or give your life to can compare to what God wants you to do for him. God's vision for you is why he created you; it is why you are on this planet.

God's Word is clear—without a vision we perish.[1] Knowing this, pastors and Christian leaders all over the world nevertheless struggle to articulate a compelling vision for their churches. A vision is important; God's vision is all-important. We need to make sure that our own vision matches his great big vision.

Let's back up a bit and find out exactly what the ultimate, big-picture vision of our heavenly Father actually looks like. Only by focusing our lives and ministries on accomplishing his vision do we succeed in realizing his will for ourselves and our churches. Let's invest in his vision rather than in our own grandiose schemes. What we think would help the cause of Christ and his kingdom falls pitifully short of God's plans. God's vision is phenomenally greater and infinitely more exciting than any vision we could ever come up with on our own.

What is the vision of God Almighty for us and his planet? Why did he create us in the first place? What is his eternal agenda for his people and his church? What is his powerful, consuming vision? Does Scripture give us any clues about his all-encompassing vision?

Thankfully, the answer is yes!

A significant hermeneutical (the rules and principles of biblical interpretation) statute is called "The Law of First Mention."[2] This is the guideline that encourages us to examine the first mention of a specific word or concept in the Bible. Often that gives us a clue to understanding how the Lord views that subject and how it *stands connected in the mind of God.*[3]

The first time the word "vision" is used in the Bible is found in Genesis 15:1—"After these things the word of the LORD came to Abram in a *vision*" (emphasis added). Of course, this is part of the Abrahamic covenant. In this first divine vision, God tells Abram that he is going to have a baby boy. From this child would come descendants too many to count, "as the stars of the heavens" (Gen. 22:17). God greatly multiplied Abraham's seed beyond anything Old Abe could imagine.

God's vision for Abram involved countless sons and daughters who would be "multiplied" to him. This included his immediate blood relatives, the descendants of Isaac (the Jews), the descendants of Ishmael, *and* spiritual children through Jesus Christ. God's ultimate vision involves the multiplication of spiritual sons and daughters to the descendants of Abraham.

Paul tells us that we Gentiles who have put our faith in Christ are the true spiritual descendants of Abraham.[4] Interestingly, in Hebrews 2:16 the author writes this wonderful promise to us: "For assuredly He does not give help to angels, but He gives help to *the descendant of Abraham*" (emphasis added). He is talking about God's born-again children, those who claim Jesus Christ as Lord and Savior. Christians, he is talking about you and me!

Through Jesus Christ, I am a "descendant of Abraham." I can both claim and count on God's help as I obey him by getting after the vision of the Father. Praise the Lord!

The very first command—remember "The Law of First Mention"—that God ever gave humans is found in Genesis 1:28: "God blessed them; and God said to them, *'Be fruitful and multiply,* and fill the earth'" (emphasis added). It is

God's decree, his founding vision, that we be fruitful and multiply.

Certainly the Lord had biological reproduction and pro-creation in mind, but is that all he was thinking about? If that is so, then what about single people such as Jesus and Paul? How can the chaste and sexually pure fulfill this command? They don't produce babies. What about couples who would love to have biological children but are barren? Our Lord meant biological multiplication, but he also meant *spiritual* multiplication. Every Christian, married or single, can be fruitful and multiply spiritual sons and daughters.

When we get to the New Testament, being fruitful and multiplying doesn't simply mean having lots of babies. It means spiritual fruit. God wants us to be totally faithful and very fruitful. Jesus taught that good soil produces a crop of good fruit that multiplies thirty times, sixty times, even one hundred times.[5] Jesus is not referring to fruitful wombs that produce huge litters of human infants. Rather, he is talking about spiritual fruit.

Jesus told us in John 15:8 that "My Father is glorified by this, that you bear *much fruit,* and so prove to be My disciples" (emphasis added). The whole thrust of John 15:1-16 is about "fruit," "more fruit," "much fruit," and "fruit that lasts."[6]

Fruit in the New Testament can refer to the fruit of the Spirit, the fruit of good works, the fruit of our lips (such as praise and thanksgiving), and the ultimate spiritual fruit that lasts—souls. If the Lord evaluated your life right now, would he declare that you have produced "much fruit" for his glory? After all, that is his vision for our lives.

Larry Stockstill says that "God's ultimate vision involves the massive multiplication of spiritual sons and daughters. It has always been in the heart and mind of God from eternity past to populate a world and later the New Jerusalem with billions of redeemed, holy, spiritual sons and daughters who obey his Word and who passionately and supremely love him eternally and worship him with all of their hearts and who will be the intimate, loving Bride of Jesus Christ forever!"[7]

To do this, God uses the wondrous, almost miraculous principle of multiplication. Addition alone won't work. Multiplication can win the entire world in one generation. Imagine if we got serious about multiplying disciples who then multiply other disciples. This exponential multiplication of disciples who make disciples could literally reach the entire population of the world in a few short years!

Spiritual multiplication starts slow and small. Initially addition is quicker, but in the end, multiplication far outstrips the greatest addition. Multiplication ushers us into the realm of unlimited, supernatural, eternal results!

Spiritual multiplication involves the personal discipling and spiritual parenting of all believers until they become spiritual parents themselves. They will reproduce spiritual children who, in time, become spiritual parents who continue reproducing new believers.

We do not truly reproduce or multiply, either biologically or spiritually, when we simply raise our children. If our children never have children themselves, then our "line" ends when they die. We reproduce only when we raise *parents* of children. This is valid in both the physical realm and the spiritual world.

Too many Christians are content only to see people find Christ. They haven't worked with these new Christians long enough or with the personal, focused intentionality that it takes to raise them into spiritual parents of other reproducing spiritual parents.

Our God is a God of multiplication. This is abundantly clear from the very first pages of his Word. His vision for us involves this reproduction. Satan is incredibly afraid of God's people who are involved in the spiritual multiplication of the disciples of Jesus!

Acts 6:1 notes that "the number of the disciples was *multiplying*" (NKJV, emphasis added). When I read that, I can't help but compare that statement with what I see in my own church. Are the people who claim to follow Christ in the church I pastor truly multiplying Christlike disciples of Jesus, or are we just coming to church and hanging out until the rapture?

It is God's vision for you and me that we multiply disciples of Jesus Christ. Is that happening in your local church? Is that an accurate description of your life and ministry? Would others be able to say of you that you are actually *multiplying disciples*?

Take a quick glance in any concordance and look up the words "multiply," "multiplied," or "multiplies." This will reveal that our dear God is constantly involved in the wondrous miracle of exponential multiplication. His blessing often involves multiplication. Consider these passages:

- Isaiah 51:2—"Look to Abraham your father, and to Sarah who gave birth to you in pain; when he was but one I called him, *then I blessed him and multiplied him*" (emphasis added).

- Genesis 9:1—"God blessed Noah and his sons and said to them, *"Be fruitful and multiply,* and fill the earth" (emphasis added).

Certainly the Lord wanted Noah and his descendants to do more than just produce more humans. God used the flood to flush the whole world of hundreds of thousands or possibly millions of violently sinful human beings.[8] He didn't want Noah and his company simply to reproduce another evil batch of corrupt people. The Lord hoped the new and succeeding generations would be spiritually holy. He longed for a loving people, sons and daughters who worshipped the Most High God. This has always been his vision for his planet and his created human beings.

- In Genesis 16:10, God promises Hagar, "I will *greatly multiply* your descendants so that they shall be too many to count" (emphasis added).

- Again in Genesis 17:2 God says to Abram, "I will establish my covenant between me and you, and I will *multiply* you exceedingly" (emphasis added).

- In addition to Abram (Abraham), God promised others that he would bless them with the miracle of multiplication. The following is only a partial list of people God said he would bless with multiplication:

  Noah—Genesis 9:1, 7

  Hagar—Genesis 16:10

  Ishmael—Genesis 17:20

  Isaac—Genesis 26:24

  Jacob (Israel)—Genesis 35:11

  Joseph—Genesis 48:16

  The Jews—Leviticus 26:9; Deuteronomy 6:3; 7:13; 8:1, 13

David—Jeremiah 33:22

The Levites—Jeremiah 33:22

Look at what else God's says he is willing to multiply to us:

- Our Lord wants to multiply his grace and peace to us —2 Peter 1:2
- God wants to multiply mercy, peace and love to us— Jude 1:2
- God desires his Word to be multiplied in and through us—Acts 12:24
- Our Heavenly Father even wants to multiply our days and years—Proverbs 9:11; Deuteronomy 11:21
- The Lord multiplied his wonders in the land of Egypt —Exodus 11:9
- God can multiply grain, fruit, the fruit of our wombs, herds, flocks, and even our spiritual seed for sowing and for harvest—Ezekiel 36:29-30; Deuteronomy 7:13; 8:13; 2 Corinthians 9:10

Most of our church growth in America is by the blessing of addition. Thank God for every soul he adds to his church, but addition is not God's primary vehicle for saving a lost and dying world. Thank the Lord for any addition growth you see in your life, ministry, or your church, yet addition growth alone will never get the job done. God wants us to bear "much fruit" for his glory. Addition is merely replacement growth.[9]

People are dying and going to hell too fast! Multiplication is God's invention, vision, and design. It's explosive exponential growth. True spiritual multiplication is God's vision for his church to reach a broken, hurting, dying world of lost men, women, boys, and girls.

God's will is that every believer becomes an effective, multiplying disciple-maker of Jesus Christ. The Great Commission of our Lord is "Go therefore and make disciples" (Matt. 28:19). This means every Christian—not just the original disciples of Jesus, not just professional missionaries and super-saints, not just pastors and Christian leaders—but every one of us. This is meant for every follower of Jesus Christ. If you are a Christian, it is God's stated will, indeed his command, for you to make disciples of Jesus. We must do everything he commanded. That, of course, means making *more disciples* who will also make more disciples of our Lord!

Can dynamic, explosive spiritual multiplication really take place in today's world? Yes! It is happening all over the globe. Consider these examples of churches around the world that are truly multiplying disciple-makers as Jesus told us to:

- A church in Lima, Peru, grew from five thousand to over thirty thousand in four years.
- A church in Kiev, Ukraine, pastored by a Nigerian grew in ten years from eight people to twenty-five thousand disciples of Jesus who are making more disciples of Jesus.
- A church in Bogota, Colombia, has grown from seven hundred to over six hundred thousand in only nineteen years. Some Sundays this church sees over five thousand come to faith in Christ. Their youth group meets in a soccer stadium that they fill twice each Saturday night with over sixty-five thousand young people in attendance.

- A church youth group in the United States grew from four hundred to over twenty-five hundred in just two years.

- A church in the United States planted over eighteen thousand churches worldwide in five years using the principles of spiritual multiplication.

- The largest Nazarene church in the world grew from thirty-one people to between twelve thousand and fourteen thousand in just thirteen years. Their weekly prayer meetings on Wednesdays now run over five thousand people who passionately call on God for souls. This church in Cali, Colombia, held a single rally in the spring of 2010 with over thirty-five thousand in attendance, and over five thousand people gave their hearts to Christ. Unbelievable, but true!

In the next chapter, this book will give you a brief overview of the Cali Nazarene story and its congregations's universal principles.

All these churches use some variation of the most explosive multiplying model of disciple-making the world has ever seen. It is known by various names around the world, but in the Church of the Nazarene we simply call it the Master's Plan.

In summary, here is the Father's vision:

- It is God's will that everybody become a born-again, Spirit-filled believer.

- It is God's will that all believers become witnesses, soul winners, and true Great Commission disciples of Jesus.

- It is God's design that every believer be discipled for life in a spiritual father/son relationship or a spiritual mother/daughter relationship.
- It is God's will that all believers become spiritual parents. They should consecutively lead others to Jesus and nurture them into full maturity in Christ.
- With God's help, a lot of prayer, and hard work by faithful disciplers, new believers should be trained to become soul winners.

Let's examine the Master's Plan and how God is using it to bring the fulfillment of the Father's vision.

 two

The Cali Story

✦ "Thirty-one," Pastor Adalberto Herrera sighed. "I hate that number." Feeling weary of the same old figure, he entered it again on the 1997 pastor's report for district assembly. The Cali, Colombia, Church of the Nazarene had bounced around between thirty and thirty-one people for twelve long years. No matter what Pastor Adalberto and his wife Nineye did, they couldn't seem to break the thirty-one barrier.

They felt discouraged, demoralized, and depressed. They had seen a few people saved and join with the church, only to watch an equal number of parishioners leave out the "back door." They tried and applied every concept and principle that the missionaries and church growth experts taught. Sadly, year after agonizing year, the Church of the Nazarene in Cali, a city of over three million, did not grow beyond that aggravating number: thirty-one!

Cali remained the drug and murder capital of the world. Surely God wanted to save the people of Cali. What was wrong? Why were other churches in their massive city seeing signs of revival and growth? Why didn't God do something? What was God's vision for the tiny Cali Church of the Nazarene? The Herreras wanted to give up on more than a few occasions. Could it be they weren't really called to this ministry?

The Cali church had been founded in 1983 by Nazarene missionary John Armstrong. The Herreras arrived that same year to assist in the planting of the new congregation. Nineye Herrera tells their story:

Our suitcases were full of dreams and expectations. We also had uncertainties when we reached Cali, Colombia. Our inexperience and lack of preparation for ministry were obvious. Still, we longed for God to do something new with us. This dream overrode the difficulties that we faced when we first arrived.

American missionary John Armstrong still led the church. During our first few months serving there, we heard someone among our small membership complain.

"Not only do we have a missionary who can't speak Spanish," the mystery voice said, "we now have a couple from the coast of Colombia who speaks so fast we can't understand them at all!"

It was true. The Colombian coastal people speak a Spanish that is characterized by very rapid speech, yet this was the humble beginning of the Nazarene work in Cali.

A tiny building was bought with Alabaster Offering funds. This building was the smallest in the entire sector. We were the target of many taunts and insults by our predominately Catholic neighbors. They looked down at us and called us the poor Evangelicals. Today we are known as the church where all the rich people go!

In 1985, the church averaged between thirty and thirty-one people. These were the numbers that we got stuck with for twelve years. In 1987, Adalberto became the senior pastor. Although we had a willing heart to serve the Lord, our ministry suffered great opposition and stagnation. We felt so discouraged.

Year after year we saw little to no progress. Finally, in 1992, Pastor Herrera cried out to God for a vision of how to make the church grow. God's answer was a simple call to prayer and fasting. Starting in 1995, every Tuesday from 4:00 a.m. until 6:00 a.m., Adalberto and I joined with three other ladies from the church in earnestly beseeching God's touch.

Later we set aside even more time on Wednesdays. Thanks be to God—he led us to this weekly time of fasting and prayer. We sought the intense presence of the Lord. On these Wednesdays we would fast from 8:00 a.m. to noon. We started with only five people, Pastor Adalberto, me, and the same three ladies who made up our original prayer group. We prayed and fasted so much that by the next year we were not five people but three. Two of our ladies moved away.

It's normal to become discouraged when you pray and fast intensely and do not see immediate results. We felt like quitting. Yet something in our hearts knew God would do mighty things in our church if we only persevered in prayer and glorified God.

We continued in prayer and fasting, but after all our work and sacrifice, we would attend the yearly district assembly only to report either thirty or thirty-one. It was devastating. We hated going to district assembly and giving this poor report. All we received for our efforts was a sense of defeat. We had serious questions regarding whether or not God had really called us to be pastors.

The only way out of our difficult situation was through prayer and fasting. Nobody on earth was interested in helping us. Our only help would come from God who made heaven and earth.

God heard our fervent cries and prayers.

Today the story is very different. Regret and sorrow have turned into great joy because God is faithful. Today our congregation is multiplying every year. To God be the glory![1]

In 1996 the Wednesday prayer meeting consisted of three people: Pastors Adalberto and Nineye and one lady. In 1997 the church was running no more than thirty-one people, but by 1998, the church had at last broken that barrier to reach forty people. The little prayer band had cried out to God, "Help us or we die!" They were desperate for God's mighty hand to move. God gave the increase, and the church soared from forty to one thousand in just a few years. This is an amazing growth for any church.

The group continued to pray and fast on Wednesdays, and the weekly prayer meeting expanded. From 2002 to 2003 the church hit a plateau at one thousand. Pastor Adalberto searched the world for a model of disciple-making that would conserve the harvest and break through the one thousand barrier.

The "back door" of the church again became as wide open as the front door. In the course of a year, several hundred accepted Christ and were added to the church, while several hundred more left out the back door, causing the church to stay at around one thousand. The prayer team searched for the Lord's wisdom on how to break through this blockade and multiply their flock.

The Cali leaders longed to see God multiply their ministry from a strong church of one thousand into *a multitude of multitudes*. After several years, the Lord graciously led them to the model that is now called the Master's Plan.

In 2003 the church implemented this comprehensive vision and strategy. In one year the church grew from one thousand to two thousand. In 2004, the Cali church went from two thousand to three thousand. God continued to bless the Master's Plan model of multiplication so that in 2005 they progressed to between five thousand and six thousand a week in their weekend attendance.

The Herreras are very clear on this point: "The Master's Plan did not bring the revival. *Prayer and fasting brought the revival.* The Master's Plan allowed us to conserve the harvest, close the back door of the church, and multiply leaders and disciple-makers. *The Master's Plan brought us into multiplication!*"

In 2005 the Lord led the Cali church to host evangelistic rallies in sports arenas and bull-fighting stadiums. In December 2005, twelve thousand attended their massive rally, where over six hundred were saved by Christ.

The church continued to multiply until, in 2006, it saw between six thousand and seven thousand at their weekend services. The prayer meetings also continued to grow. Tuesday prayer groups generally ran from 4:00 a.m. until 7:00 a.m., and the three Wednesday prayer gatherings stretched from 6:00 a.m. to 9:00 a.m., from 9:00 a.m. to noon, and from 7:00 p.m. to 10:00 p.m. Round-the-clock teams of intercessors cried out to God for revival and for souls at the church seven days a week and 365 days a year.

God heard their cries and phenomenally answered their prayers. In 2007 the church expanded to between seven thousand and eight thousand. They reached fourteen thousand at their sports arena rally and joyfully watched as eleven hundred gave their hearts to the Lord.

In 2008, the once-tiny Cali church averaged nine thousand people each weekend. During that year they held two evangelistic rallies of hope and salvation. At one of these meetings eighteen thousand attended, while another three thousand couldn't fit inside the arena and thus listened outside the stadium, eager to hear God's message. Over twelve hundred were born again. In the other arena gathering, fourteen thousand attended and nine hundred found their way into the Kingdom.

In 2009, the Nazarene church in Cali typically had ten thousand weekend worshippers. Their now-annual arena convention witnessed over twenty thousand gathered to praise God and hear his gospel powerfully proclaimed. The church reported over fifteen hundred who responded to their evangelistic invitation in only one great day of harvest!

In 2010, they regularly had between twelve thousand and fourteen thousand at their six weekend meetings. The sanctuary is standing-room-only in all six services. In order to meet the needs of their community, two more services were scheduled to begin before Christmas 2010, with leaders expecting them to fill up rapidly.

In their spring 2010 evangelistic rally, over thirty-five thousand were in attendance. At the conclusion, more than five thousand prayed to receive Christ. That's two thousand more than were saved in the Acts 2 original day of Pentecost!

Here's the truly remarkable logistical accomplishment. Those five thousand people each received a phone call within twenty-four hours of the event. Then, all five thousand received a personal visit within forty-eight hours of Sunday's service. Next, all five thousand were personally contacted and invited to life groups within a short distance of their homes, regardless of where in that great city they lived.

This is where it really gets exciting! If the projections hold true to the averages the Cali church is presently enjoying, then somewhere in the neighborhood of eighty percent of those new converts will be retained in the church. Furthermore, fifty percent will complete the Master's Plan training and become disciple-makers. Within a year they will lead their own small groups. Realistically, they are looking at having twenty-five hundred new small groups within a year of their major event. This is multiplication.

Another rally was planned for September 2010. The church prayed, believed, and worked hard to see forty-five thousand not only attend, but also come under the influence of the gospel and the power of Jesus Christ. Only God knows what will be the result of their concerted, focused effort.

All of this is powered by fervent, intercessory prayer and fasting. Wednesday is a day of fasting for the entire church. Round-the-clock intercession continues at the church 365 days a year. As of September 2010, the three prayer meetings are averaging:

6:00 a.m.-9:00 a.m.	1,800
9:00 a.m.-noon	1,200
7:00 p.m.-10:00 p.m.	2,000
Total	5,000

The church in Cali has purchased property to build a new, seven-thousand-seat sanctuary that will cost over eleven million United States dollars. Miraculously, the church has already raised five million dollars. The church is praying fervently for the remaining balance.

The Nazarenes of Cali, Colombia, expect to fill their new coliseum multiple times each weekend. This is the harvest of souls that God granted them through their prayers, fasting, and use of the Master's Plan of disciple-making. God keeps on multiplying the disciples in Cali, Colombia. The pastoral team believes the Lord is just getting warmed up and they expect some truly amazing wonders in their city. The church remains in constant prayer, trusting God for one hundred thousand to attend their weekend services.

Don't forget—just thirteen years ago, in 1998, this church struggled to break the thirty-one barrier. What can God do with you and a small group of Christians willing to fervently pray and obey his command to make disciples of Jesus who will make yet more disciples of Jesus? You'll be amazed at the wonders and glory of God.

When God multiplies—stand back! The Cali story is just getting started. They are planting churches using this same dynamic model and have trained several thousand pastors in the Master's Plan. The multiplication story has only begun to be written.

three

What Is the Master's Plan?

⤙ The Master's Plan is the Church of the Nazarene's adaptation of the explosive disciple-making model that is known worldwide by the nickname "G12."

What Does G12 Stand For?

G12 is shorthand for a government of twelve. In biblical numerology, twelve is the number typically representing order, discipline, blessing, multiplication, government, or organization. After some adaptation and theological adjustments, the Church of the Nazarene called this scriptural, Wesleyan model the Master's Plan.

Who Uses This Model of Discipleship?

Over thirty thousand churches worldwide, including over three thousand churches in North America, use this model of disciple-making. It is employed in the largest churches in virtually every country in the world. Over 125 different denominations, most of them charismatic, embrace this model's principles. It is also taught by over fifty Churches of the Nazarene in Central and South America as well as over one hundred Nazarene churches in North America.

Where Did This Model Come From?

In 1991, God gave the Master's Plan to a charismatic pastor from Bogota, Colombia, named Cesar Castellanos. A Methodist scholar and author named Robert Coleman introduced Castellanos and his staff to this Wesleyan model several decades ago. Since using the model, the Bogota church has gone from seven hundred to over six hundred thousand worshippers.

After close examination, it's easy for any Wesleyan scholar to see how this model was originally used by John Wesley. His earliest Methodists practiced an interlocking system of small groups that included class meetings, bands, and select societies. The Master's Plan is a modern retrofitting of the effective small group disciple-making that John Wesley believed was essential to personal growth in holiness and accountability in personal purity.

The charismatics borrowed this model from John Wesley, but now we Wesleyan Nazarenes are gladly reclaiming our spiritual heritage and legacy of holiness and accountability.

What Are the Basic Components of This Model?

1. A powerful, anointed Encounter Weekend Retreat is offered in which Christians are invited to have a true life-changing encounter with God. They have a chance to be sanctified by God's Spirit.

2. Then, a year's worth of weekly classes are offered in practical holiness. They are designed to lead newly sanctified Christians to the point at which they become true disciples of our Lord Jesus. Next, these disciples are trained to become reproducing disciple-makers. Less than a year after their conversion, these Christians find themselves both equipped and encouraged to lead their own small groups. They will disciple others while they continue receiving ongoing coaching and mentoring.

3. Next, a constant, small group of committed believers will meet weekly in prayer. They'll unite in asking God for mutual support, praying for lost people and giving encouragement to those who are learning to apply God's Word. Some churches call them life groups, small groups, cell groups, or TLC groups. For our purposes, we'll call them life groups. They range from three to twenty-five people and can be same-sex or mixed-gender gatherings. These evangelistic life groups are *open* meetings in the sense that anyone and everyone is welcome to attend. Typically they meet weekly for a little over an hour.

4. The long-term, one-on-one coaching, mentoring, and same-sex discipling now results in Christlike disciples who are weekly accountable to other disciplers. They have been transformed into disciple-makers themselves.

5. Disciplers are a part of a lead group. This is a *closed* group of believers who are the leaders of small groups that never grow beyond twelve people. The lead group meets for prayer, encouragement, accountability, and strategizing. Typically these are same-sex groups. Some churches call them groups of 12, leaders' groups, G12 groups, or simply closed groups. They gather weekly for one and a half to two hours.

6. Eventually, each leader has his or her own weekly lead group of faithful leaders whom he or she is discipling and coaching into fruitful maturity in Christ.

This model is sweeping the world while revolutionizing discipling, spiritual formation, and church planting. Its vision, passion, lifestyle, mind-set, and methodology have been effectively implemented by the fastest-growing churches in the world today. In 2010, Jerry Porter reported that it is now used by the largest churches in every country on planet earth.[1]

Many believe this is the most explosive, dynamic, multiplying model of disciple-making the world has seen since the time of the book of Acts. Dr. Paul David Yonggi Cho of Korea is pastor of the world's largest church. With over a million people in his congregation, he declared publicly that this particular model of spiritual reproduction and intensive discipling is one that "can revolutionize and empower the church all over the world to take cities and nations for God."[2] Numerous pastors who agree with Dr. Cho are witnessing their churches multiplying.

This is a *cell church* vision. Nineteen of the twenty largest churches in the world are cell churches. A cell church is not just a church with cells. In a true cell church, *cells* are not the same as home groups, care groups, fellowship groups, Bible study groups, prayer groups, service groups, or affinity groups. It's a church where the whole movement, thrust, life, and ministry operate in and through cells of believing Christians.

Colin Dye of Kensington Temple in London writes, "Rather, they are tiny units of 'church' doing everything that 'church' should be doing while remaining part of the overall body. Cells are where the evangelism, discipleship, pastoral care and prayer life of the church takes place."[3]

The vision and mandate of the Master's Plan are found in the way Jesus Christ ministered to and through his twelve disciples. Pastor Dye believes that, "Based on the way Jesus chose and trained twelve disciples, The Master's Plan vision is proving to be the most effective way of equipping the body of Christ in the world today. Its goal is to see every member of the body of Christ serving the Lord Jesus and fulfilling his mandate to make, mature and mobilize disciples in all nations."[4]

Pastor Cesar Castellanos, mentioned earlier, felt so discouraged that his church couldn't grow beyond 120 people that he officially resigned. Frustrated, he prepared his heart to wait on God to show him what to do next. Over the next four months, he remained in prayer before the Lord.

Through a series of visions, God revealed to Pastor Castellanos a strategy of evangelism and church growth through cells. In 1986, he went to Korea and adopted the principles of the cell church as taught by Dr. Cho.

By the end of 1991, he had seventy cells and roughly seven hundred people in the church. Pastor Castellanos was not content. He earnestly cried out to the Lord for a plan to accelerate the growth of cells and leaders. He believed the Lord had showed him the missing component—the Master's Plan.

Castellanos writes, "I began to see Jesus' ministry with clarity. The multitudes followed, but he didn't train the multitudes. He only trained twelve, and everything he did with the multitudes was for the purpose of teaching the twelve. Then the Lord asked me another question: 'If Jesus trained twelve, should *you* win with more than twelve or less than twelve?'"[5]

The Lord continued showing Pastor Castellanos how Jesus chose twelve to reach the multitudes. As he further studied the life and ministry of Jesus, he realized that Jesus permanently stayed with these twelve disciples until they were trained. Only then did he release them, give them authority, and empower them to disciple the nations.

The call to Castellanos's heart rang clear: find twelve faithful men, and by the Spirit of God, reproduce Christ's character in them. His wife Claudia copied his example with twelve women of the church. His youth pastor and brother-in-law, Cesar Fajardo, did the same thing with the church's youth. Each of these twelve, in turn, won, discipled, and sent out twelve more.

Soon 12 became 144, which grew to 1,728, which expanded to 20,736. God promised them unprecedented growth if they obeyed the vision he had given.

This resulted in unbelievable multiplication. From 1991 to 1994, his church's cells grew from 70 to 1,200. Then from 1994 to 1999 occurred an explosion of growth to twenty thousand cells with forty-five thousand people meeting on the weekends for celebration services. In 1996, the cells expanded from 4,000 to 10,500. Each cell held between six and twenty-five people.[6] Today over six hundred thousand are discipled in almost one hundred thousand cells. Each of these six hundred thousand is being groomed to lead his or her own cells.

In the Master's Plan, churches firmly believe that every Christian can and should be trained for life as a successful cell leader. The International Charismatic Mission church in Bogota, Colombia, truly believes that in a year or two they will have six hundred thousand cells, each averaging four to five worshippers.

This church continues to explode with exponential growth. Today, nineteen years after God gave Castellanos the vision of ministering to twelve men, over six hundred thousand are discipled by leaders. All of them are training to be soul-winners, disciplers and leaders of twelve. The youth group alone reaches sixty-five thousand youth who, on some weekends, lead over fifteen hundred teens to Christ.

Many weekends the church in Bogota has five thousand people come to salvation in Christ. Their retention rate is the envy of every church in the world at eighty to ninety percent of their first-time converts. Nearly sixty-five percent of these new believers participate in the year-long training to become cell group leaders.

This is nothing short of miraculous. Amazingly, it is reproducible and transfers easily to other cultures and countries. As stated earlier, this movement has spread over the world, is found on every continent but Antarctica, and has been implemented by over thirty thousand churches worldwide. Over 124 denominations in East Africa alone use this model of disciple multiplication.

In Baton Rouge, Louisiana, Larry Stockstill pastored the Bethany World Prayer Center. They ran five thousand members when they began applying this model's principles and philosophy. At that time, they were retaining only six percent of their new converts. That was in 2001, nine years ago. Today they average in excess of thirteen thousand members with two hundred first-time converts every week. Better still, they retain over fifty percent of these new believers. The leadership of Bethany is convinced that this is due to this multiplying model and the methodology of consolidation and discipleship.

In 2003, Bethany's youth group ran four hundred. They moved their youth group into a full implementation of the Master's Plan and today run over five thousand in weekly cell group meetings led, for the most part, by other teens. This is the largest youth group in America by at least three thousand![7]

Most megachurches in America have youth groups that run "only" about three hundred to five hundred young people. Only three or four megachurches see over one thousand kids, making Bethany the largest by far. Their leaders truly expect a youth group of twenty thousand someday. This is in the United States!

Bethany is a very mission-minded church, having given two to three million dollars to missions for several years. For the fifteen years between 1987 and 2003 they planted one thousand churches worldwide. Not bad for one American church!

In 2003 they moved all one thousand of these churches to this multiplying model. In 2004 they planted another two thousand or more churches. They followed this in 2005 when they planted over six thousand churches worldwide. Every one of them uses this program.

Currently this church is planting ten thousand churches a year using this dynamic strategy. Each pastor is charged with raising up his or her 12, their 144, their 1,728, and so on. They will plant new churches using this explosive methodology. In comparison, as of 2010 in the one hundred two years of the Church of the Nazarene's existence, the denomination has started some eighteen thousand churches worldwide.[8]

 four

The Encounter Weekend Retreat

✦ The Master's Plan is much more than a batch of curriculum or a mere program. It is a lifestyle, a passion, and a guideline that includes clear objectives. While providing us a life-changing blueprint complete with classes and events, it also gives us a direction that can easily be followed.

One of the significant events in the Master's Plan is the Encounter Weekend Retreat. This is foundational and fundamental to everything else that goes on in the Master's Plan. Without the Encounter Weekend Retreat, the Master's Plan would be just another study program or curriculum. Typically in a church just starting the Master's Plan, the order of events is as follows:

1. The pastor prays through the Master's Plan until he or she senses God's clear call into this model. This is a vital step. Don't attempt the Master's Plan without this critical component. The senior pastor *must* know that God has clearly called him or her into this powerful, all-encompassing itinerary.

2. The pastor leads his or her board or leadership team into *buying into* the Master's Plan. This may involve a trip to Cali, Colombia, to attend their excellent annual conference. Traveling to Nazarene churches in North America that successfully implement this mod-

el is also beneficial. A number of Nazarene churches train other pastors and leaders. Both the pastor and his or her spouse should attend a Nazarene Encounter Weekend Retreat before attempting to hold one of their own.

3. The first years are filled with intense soul preparation and focused intercession by the pastor and leaders of the church. During this time, the pastor and his select team closely study the Master's Plan. Books, CDs, DVDs, and conferences are available to help a leadership team grasp everything involved in this dynamic model. Some churches bring in an established Master's Plan leader to provide coaching in this world-changing vision.

4. A year or two is devoted to establishing a strong prayer base in the local church. The importance of this groundwork cannot be overstated. Churches that don't get prayer support established will surely fail.

5. The pastor prayerfully and carefully selects a leadership team to go through their first Encounter Weekend Retreat.

6. A pre-Encounter training session for all participants is required, which runs anywhere from four to six hours before the Encounter Weekend Retreat is held. At the pre-Encounter, the participants are told what to expect at the Encounter, what to bring, and what not to bring. Coaching is given on preparing the heart for an encounter with God. Questions and concerns are addressed. Some preliminary teaching is given on sanctification and other topics that they will come across at the Encounter. Fears are alleviated. Prayer

is offered concerning the upcoming event. A spirit of joyful anticipation is cultivated. Pre-Encounters are very important in preparing hearts for what the Lord will do. Churches that omit this vital step inevitably regret it.

7. The Encounter Weekend Retreat is experienced. The Lord honors us with his phenomenal presence. At the retreat, we encounter God and he encounters us. Lives are changed. People are set free and marvelously sanctified. The vision of the Master's Plan is cast before the participants at the Encounter. People leave the Encounters exhausted, but excited about the upcoming process of disciple training.

What Happens at the Encounter Weekend Retreat?

It is an intense weekend revival that can be held at a hotel, retreat center, or even the local church. Ideally, we recommend your group gets away to a hotel or a retreat setting. With the costs involved, however, this isn't always possible. Many churches are successfully doing Encounters using their own churches as *in-house* retreats. It is not best, but it works.

The leadership of the church takes part in much prayer and fasting before the retreat. Each session is covered in intercessory prayer by prayer teams. Typically the Encounter begins on a Friday evening. A meal on the premises is provided, followed by an introduction and worship session. We enter each Encounter expecting God to show up and dramatically move in all of us. Then, one or two teaching sessions are held that first evening.

The Encounter will bring a revival. We will encounter God. The Lord never disappoints. He unites with us and deals with our very diverse needs. We are never the same again.

The next day, Saturday, starts bright and early with worship and teaching-preaching sessions. There are typically ten of these that run anywhere from a half hour to one hour. A session has a prayer activity at the conclusion. Each participant responds to what the Lord tells him or her, yielding to God various levels of his or her life.

These go on all day with appropriate breaks for mealtime on the premises and some small-group activities and prayer. Some groups end on Saturday evening around 8:00 or 9:00 p.m. Other churches continue on and make it a full forty-four- to forty-eight-hour retreat ending on Sunday afternoon.

Here is a list of what is covered in the classes:

1. **The Prodigal Son**

   A strong presentation of the Heavenly Father's love and forgiveness.

2. **A Face-to-Face Encounter with God**

   The story of Jacob at Peniel and his surrender to God. He meets God and wrestles with him all night. We allow God to break us so that he can bless and use us.

3. **The Power of the Cross**

   Here we take a fresh look at the crucifixion of Christ and the nailing of our sins to the cross. This serves as a reminder of what it cost Jesus to redeem us. This moving session is followed by a small-group communion.

4. **The Power of the Resurrection**

   The emphasis is on daily walking in Christ's resurrection life and power.

5. **Sexual Purity**

   A strong challenge to walk in sexual purity in all areas of our lives.

6. **The Power of Forgiveness**

   The vital lesson in this session is the importance and power of forgiving others and ourselves.

7. **Inner Healing**

   An emotional heart healing from old wounds is experienced.

8. **Set Free**

   The believer finds deliverance from all bondage and demonic influence or oppression. He or she experiences the glory of God. Strong spiritual warfare is conducted. An emphasis is made on the importance of daily being in God's presence.

9. **Baptism by the Holy Spirit and Entire Sanctification**

   A clear call is given for believers to be truly sanctified. This is followed by an opportunity to be filled with the Holy Spirit.

10. **Our Destiny—The Vision and Strategy**

    The Master's Plan overview. God's plan to make us all disciple-makers is presented in a compelling call. An opportunity is given for people to sign up for and commit themselves to the year's worth of classes.

Each Encounter participant sits throughout the retreat with a small group of three to five same-sex believers and a trained guide. These guides are each fervently praying for the members of his or her small group. These leaders are prepared to lovingly listen to and coach them. Often for days or even weeks before the retreat the guides pray over the list of names of those who will be in their small group. Typically revival has already come to the heart of the guides *before* the Encounter takes place. They come very excited about what the Lord is about to do. This spirit of joyful anticipation is an element of faith that God honors with his presence in powerful dimensions.

As mentioned earlier, at the conclusion of each session an opportunity is given in each Encounter group for prayer and confession to God. Individual participants share what God is doing within them. Wonderful, life-changing things happen in these small groups. Souls are transformed before our eyes.

Layer after layer, the Holy Spirit does his wonderful work. People are hungry for each new step. All of this leads to the opportunity to be truly sanctified. This is followed by a challenge to get personally discipled in holiness and disciple-making. They're offered training to fulfill the Great Commission, Matthew 28:18-20.

God moves among us as we minister to one another in a spirit of brokenness, humility, confession, and prayer. James 5:16 says, "Confess your sins to one another, and pray for one another so that you may be healed. The effective prayer of a righteous man can accomplish much." All this and more happens at an Encounter Weekend Retreat.

No one at these retreats is forced to confess anything publicly, yet as the Holy Spirit moves across the room, people inevitably share from their heart to the members of their trusted small groups. Tears flow, people get right with God, believers are sanctified, and the Holy Spirit falls on people at these intense retreats. Jesus is glorified. Spiritual warfare takes place. Victories are won and reported. The Lord conquers any force hindering his people from fully following and serving him in joy, humility, and obedience. It is a genuine wonder. God's people worship him.

Encounters are impossible to fully describe to someone who has never attended one. They have to be experienced to be understood. God is doing marvelous things in our Encounters. People all across the world are set free and entirely sanctified. Glory to his name!

We live in an age when people in North America have become too busy to attend traditional camp meetings, which can go on for a week. Far too many Nazarenes are too consumed with modern life to attend every night of even a four-day revival meeting at their local church. The Encounter Retreat is less than forty-eight hours. It contains ten concentrated, highly focused, powerfully anointed preaching-teaching sessions that result in real spiritual growth, change, and renewal.

Encounters are designed only for believers. It's created to take a new Christian, or even an older one, into a higher commitment with our God. They find personal forgiveness, purity, obedience, victory, and entire sanctification. We expect and see supernatural deliverances along with phenomenal healings of bodies, souls, hearts, and spirits. God is wonderfully blessing this vehicle. He encounters us, and we leave truly changed.

While we encourage only believers to attend an Encounter Retreat, not surprisingly, some unbelievers sneak in under the radar. By attending the Encounter, they are gloriously saved. We can't seem to stop this from happening—as if we wanted to. Praise the Lord!

This, in a nutshell, is what happens at the Master's Plan Encounter Weekend Retreats. There is much more we could share about what happens. In fact, a whole book could be filled with the moving testimonies of Nazarenes who have seen their lives incredibly altered at an Encounter Weekend Retreat.

 five

The Courses and Classes of the Master's Plan

✦ In the Master's Plan, our goal is to take new believers in Jesus Christ to the Encounter Weekend Retreat. There they are gloriously set free, sanctified, and filled with the Holy Spirit. Then we engage them in a year of courses resulting in these new believers becoming effective disciple-makers of Jesus Christ.

We have all witnessed the tragic phenomenon of people being wondrously saved and sanctified only to fall away from their commitment to Jesus in a few short months. These classes are designed to build upon the thrilling, sanctification event with a process of growth and development. It is personal, practical holiness that moves the young believer into paths of maturity and fruitfulness and gives a sense of excitement over beginning his or her multiplication for the glory of our God. These lessons are a part of the post-Encounter process that results in disciple-makers who multiply disciples of Jesus.

We are no longer satisfied to witness new Christians undergoing a life-changing experience with God at an Encounter Weekend Retreat only to watch them wither on the vine. Unfruitfulness, lukewarmness, and unfaithfulness eventually move them into a backslidden state. This is not the will of God, and it is not our will either. God wants each new Christian parented, coached, or mentored into Christlikeness and fruitful disciple-making.

What process did the earliest disciples of Jesus go through as they journeyed with him? They were personally taught disciple-making by God's Son. Can we learn anything from their three-year intensive training school? What stages of development did they undergo in order to evolve into effective disciples of Christ? How can it happen with us also?

The apostles of Jesus were first unbelievers, of course. They became believers as Christ ministered on the earth. By the time of his death on the cross, there were multitudes of believers.

From that throng of believers were hundreds who grew into truly devoted followers of Jesus. These were more than simply believers—they were committed *followers*. Some literally followed him around the countryside, such as the women in Luke 8. Some, such as Mary, Martha, and Lazarus of Bethany, were followers of our Lord but did not travel with him. They stayed in one location, faithfully following his teachings. From these pools of followers, Jesus hand-picked his twelve disciples.

Jesus interacted with those around him. They witnessed his miracles and listened to his teachings. Soon they became true believers. The great process had begun. Christ moved them closer, deliberately placing them in his inner circle.

As believers, each of the twelve later became his followers. From his hundreds of followers, Jesus called only a few to be his disciples. Today, Jesus calls *all* of us to be more than just believers and followers; he calls *all* of us to be his disciples.

For our purposes, we'll distinguish between the followers and disciples of Jesus. Today many are followers of Christ, but relatively few are true *disciples* of our Lord. In Scripture, these two terms are often used interchangeably, but there is a distinction between people who are followers and those who move closer to him. They cross into our Lord's inner circle, developing into devoted disciples of Jesus.

By definition, disciples are *disciplined learners* of a leader, master, or teacher. They passionately want to imitate their leader. Our churches are full of people who would classify themselves as believers or followers of Jesus. They believe in the Bible and the Christian creeds. They definitely want to go to heaven someday. Sadly, few of them are actual disciplined learners. They are far from being eager imitators of Christ.

As *disciplined learners*, the disciples listened to Jesus—they learned of him and from him. They felt continually challenged to become his servants. They desired to serve him by serving each other as well as their hurting world. Jesus told them that those who wanted to be great leaders among them needed to become everybody else's slave.[1]

Jesus continually modeled the virtue of a servant who genuinely loved to serve others. On that last night in the upper room, he provided his disciples with an example by washing their feet and then encouraging them to be servants to one another. That same night, the disciples had once again argued over who was the greatest in their group. Each man no doubt nominated himself.

They still hadn't caught the basic lesson in servanthood. Jesus wanted to send them out to become multiplying disciple-makers, but he knew they really weren't ready. The disciples had to be purged of their basic selfish carnality.

Only when the disciples grew into selfless, sacrificial servants would they be prepared for the next step. Jesus had to wait to release them to reproduce disciples. They would finally become disciple-makers—but only after being sanctified. They first needed to get saturated with his Spirit, his purity, his passion, and his power. This happened at Pentecost.

So Jesus gave them his next-to-last command: the Great Commission, found in Matthew 28:18-20. He provided them this great assignment and then added another mandate, his last one, strangely commanding them *not* to go just yet. They were to first wait for something else to happen.

Jesus knew that they needed one thing more—the cleansing and power of the Holy Spirit. They must be filled with God's purifying, empowering presence. Only the indwelling, sanctifying power of the Holy Spirit could change these first disciples into the sacrificing, selfless servants who would love and serve everybody just like Jesus. They needed his Holy Spirit to give them his perfect, pure love so they could truly be his servants.

The last command Jesus gave was "Before you go—wait!"

Wait for the promise of the Father. Wait for the baptism with the Holy Spirit. Wait for the fire that brings them the power, the purity, and the passion to be servants. Wait for God's sanctifying strength to serve a lost and dying world that would reject them, despise them, and kill them.

Once they received sanctification to be servants of our Lord, then Jesus trusted them with the vital business of multiplying. They reproduced disciple-makers all over the world.

Jesus knew we teach what we know but reproduce what we are. He wanted his disciples to become servants—true servants whom he could empower to make disciples of the nations. His disciples would finally be like him, just as their disciples would become like them. They had to be pure. They had to be cleansed of their selfishness. They had to be empowered to live holy, anointed lives. They had to reproduce and multiply disciples in their reflected image of Christ.

So Jesus gave them his command to "go and make disciples" (see Matt. 28:19). This must become our top priority. Then he gave his last command: "Wait until the Spirit falls on you" (see Luke 24:49; Acts 1:4).

This must become our first order of each and every day. We cannot successfully go until we have waited. We must receive a fresh baptism of the Holy Spirit every day. We cannot make disciples of Jesus until we tarry for a fresh, daily filling of his Holy Spirit—our efforts will ultimately be futile. Instead of making disciples of Jesus, we will merely make little pathological clones of ourselves, and we do indeed clone our own pathologies and carnalities—but who wants that?

We want everybody we know, everybody in our community and everybody in our churches, to move from being unbelievers to becoming believers in Jesus. We also want so much more. We strongly desire that everybody move from being an unbeliever to becoming a

born-again believer in Jesus, then a

faithful follower of Jesus, then a

disciplined disciple of Jesus, then a

sanctified servant of Jesus, then a

dedicated disciple-maker of Jesus, and finally a

devoted disciple-maker of disciple-makers of Jesus!

The Master's Plan is designed to help a new person go through these various stages.

The Master's Plan Timeline

COURSES	MEET	TIME	DURATION
The Believer's Course			
Pre-Encounter Classes	Weekly	1 to 1½ hour	1 month
Encounter Weekend Retreat	Quarterly	10 sessions or as needed	Weekend retreat
Post-Encounter Classes			
Follower's Course	Weekly	1½ hours	3 months
Disciple's Course	Weekly	1½ hours	3 months
Servant's Course	Weekly	1½ hours	3 months
Re-Encounter Weekend Retreat	9 mo. after the Encounter	11 sessions	Weekend Retreat
Disciple-Maker's Course	Weekly	1½ hours	3 months

Our goal: A taught, trained, and prepared soul winner ready to reproduce and multiply—winning others and starting them through the entire process.

The Believer's Course

When someone is won to the Lord, having moved from being an unbeliever to being a born-again believer in Jesus, there's an immediate follow-up with a trained worker. Together they once more discuss the plan of salvation and pray. The worker gives the new believer assurances of salvation and records his or her name, address, email address, phone number, and any specific prayer requests. A Bible is provided to the person if needed. Follow-up continues with a next-day phone call and an in-home visit within the first seventy-two hours.

Personal follow-up continues with a same-sex mentor who teaches the new believer by using resources like the eight-week lessons of Chic Shaver's *Basic Bible Studies*. These classes are specifically designed for new Christians.

Then the believer's three-component course can begin. The new believer is first invited into a life group, preferably in the company of the person who led him or her to the Lord or even one with his or her follow-up worker. They meet weekly for fellowship, encouragement in God's Word, evangelism, and prayer for both their needs and those of their lost friends.

Everyone is welcome to a life group, regardless of whether or not they are believers. These groups are open and run from three to twenty-five people. Weekly attendance and involvement in a life group is strongly encouraged for the new believer. These gatherings are their lifelines, and members quickly become a spiritual family. These groups are evangelistic—they pray for souls, and they lead people to Christ.

Next the new believer is encouraged to attend the believer's pre-Encounter classes. These prepare them for the Encounter Weekend Retreat.

The Believer's Pre-Encounter Classes

Four one-hour sessions

This is the prerequisite for the Encounter Weekend Retreat and can take place over four weeks or in one extended Saturday afternoon-evening session.

There are seven lessons in the pre-Encounter classes:

1. A Great Decision. *Following Christ, becoming a Christian, and basic follow-up.*
2. Water Baptism.
3. Communion with God. *Fellowship with the Father.*
4. The Power of the Cross. *What Christ's wounds and blood secured for us.*

5. The Baptism with the Holy Spirit and Entire Sanctification.

6. The Importance of Encountering God. *What happens when we experience a true encounter with the living God.*

7. Preparation for Your Encounter. *Guidelines for the Encounter Weekend.*

The third and final step in the believer's course is to attend the Encounter Weekend, as discussed in chapter 4.

The Follower's Course

Three months of one-and-a-half-hour sessions

This post-Encounter class is designed to help the believer who has gone through the Encounter Weekend Retreat grow into more than a mere believer. He or she learns to be a faithful follower of Jesus. These classes build on the foundation laid down at the Encounter Weekend Retreat.

Classes include material on basic biblical doctrines, practical daily holiness, and establishing dynamic daily meetings with Jesus. What does it mean to actually be a follower of the Lord Jesus Christ? How do we do that? These scriptural lessons explain exactly what a follower of Jesus does and how he or she lives.

Assignments include weekly Bible memorization and reading the New Testament through in three months. At the conclusion of this three-month quarter, the student has a good knowledge of what the Word demands of a faithful follower of our Lord.

The growing follower of Jesus is encouraged to maintain attendance in his or her life group for weekly support and prayer.

There are ten sessions in the follower's course:

1. The Victory and Power of the Cross in Our Daily Lives.
2. Meeting with Jesus. *Basics on establishing a time with Jesus and an introduction to daily prayer.*
3. Getting into God's Word.
4. The Holy Spirit.
5. Overcoming Temptation.
6. Memorizing God's Word.
7. How to Listen to Jesus, Parts 1-3.
8. How to Tell Somebody About Jesus.
9. The Importance of Life Groups and God's Family.
10. More than a Believer: A Follower of Jesus.

The Disciple's Course

Three months of one-and-a-half-hour sessions

The next level of classes helps the follower of Jesus develop into *more than a follower.* He or she becomes a disciplined disciple of Jesus. Classes include material on Bible doctrine, practical Christian family life, and what it means to be a true disciplined learner. This is the very definition of a disciple. Assignments include reading and weekly Bible memorization. During this next three-month quarter, participants again read the entire New Testament.

The developing disciple of Jesus continues attending his or her life group, adding three more people to the life group he or she attends during the three months. The disciple prepares to someday launch his or her own life group. This is valuable observation time for the disciple of Christ who is transforming into a disciple-maker.

There are ten to thirteen sessions in the disciple's course. In each are two lessons. The first is on doctrine or biblical truth. The second is on the practical principles of a godly family.

Biblical Truth Lessons

The first forty-five minutes of each session

1. Introduction to the Disciple's Course. *The definition of a disciple—more than a follower, a disciplined student. The disciple's foundation.*

2. The Disciple's Bible. *The importance of the Word of God as the disciple's food and source of strength, sword and nourishment.*

3. The Disciple's Repentance or Mind-set. *Change of mind.*

4. The Disciple's New Birth.

5. The Disciple's Faith. *The importance of faith in the life of a disciple.*

6. The Disciple's Baptisms. *Water baptism and the baptism of the Holy Spirit.*

7. The Disciple's Authority. *Laying-on of hands.*

8. The Disciple's Resurrection and Judgment.

9. The Disciple's Power. *Principles of prayer.*

10. The Disciple's Financial Freedom.

11. The Disciple's Victory.

12. The Disciple's Life. *What God's Word says about being a true disciple of Jesus. Levels of Christian commitment, maturity, and discipling.*

13. The Disciple's Life Group and the Prayer of Three, Part 1.

Lessons on the Practical Principles of a Godly Family

The second forty-five minutes of each session in the disciple's course

1. Introduction to God's Design for the Disciple's Family.
2. The Disciple's Family. *Roles in the family.*
3. The Disciple's Children.
4. The Disciple's Communication in the Family.
5. The Disciple's Intimacy within the Family. *Family intimacy and oneness.*
6. The Disciple's Finances. *Managing money God's way.*
7. The Disciple's Resolving of Conflicts.
8. The Disciple's Family Bonding.
9. The Disciple's Family Ministering Together.
10. The Disciple's Family. *Keeping it all in balance.*
11. The Disciple's Winning Witness. *Important principles in winning our friends to Jesus.*
12. The Disciple's Life Group and the Prayer of Three, Part 2.
13. Life as a Devoted Disciple of Jesus.

The Servant's Course

Three months of one-and-a-half-hour sessions

The servant's course is designed to further grow the disciple of Christ into an unselfish, sanctified servant. He or she will lead by serving others as did Jesus. The original twelve disciples needed training by our Lord in order to become genuine Christlike servants. They had to learn how to delight in ministering to others. Putting another's needs ahead of their own ambitions and desires wasn't always easy.

The courses include further biblical teaching into the heart and vision of the Father for his world. They also provide training in servanthood, life groups, evangelism, spiritual warfare, intercession, and counseling new believers.

After an interview with the pastor, the growing, sanctified servant of Jesus launches his or her own life group. During this three-month period, he or she attends the Re-Encounter Weekend Retreat for servant leaders.

Assignments include reading, weekly Bible memorization, active sharing of faith with unbelievers, and for the third time since the Encounter, reading the entire New Testament.

There are ten to thirteen sessions in the servant's course. There are two lessons in each session. The first lesson in each session helps the servant of Jesus to understand the Father's heart and vision for the world and the second is about the servant's role in God's plan to redeem his lost children.

Lessons on Biblical Truth

The first forty-five minutes of each session
of the servant's course

1. Introduction: God's Vision for the World and His Plan for His Servants.
2. The Four Faces of the Vision, Part 1. *Ezekiel's divine vision and how it relates to being a servant of Jesus. The ox, the man, the eagle, the lion.*
3. The Four Faces of the Vision, Part 2.
4. The Servant's Vision.

5. The Servant's Life Group. *The biblical basis of life groups.*

6. The Servant's Multiplication. *The seven secrets of a multiplying life. Faithful servants multiply.*

7. How to Serve a New Christian and Follow Up on Him or Her, Part 1.

8. How to Serve a New Christian and Follow Up on Him or Her, Part 2.

9. How to Serve a New Christian and Follow Up on Him or Her, Part 3.

10. How to Serve a New Christian and Follow Up on Him or Her, Part 4.

11. God's Servant and the Power of Small.

12. God's Vision for the Future for His Selfless Servants: Fantastic Fruitfulness, Part 1.

13. God's Vision for the Future for His Selfless Servants: Fantastic Fruitfulness, Part 2.

Lessons on the Practical Principles of Ministry

The second forty-five minutes of each session
of the servant's course

1. Introduction. The Servant's Ministry. *Discovering your ministry.*

2. The Servant's Ministry to God. *Praise and worship.*

3. The Servant's Warfare. *Spiritual warfare.*

4. The Servant's Intercession and Supplication. *Prayer and life groups.*

5. The Servant's Ministry in the Life Group. *The value of a life group.*

6. The Servant's Ministry in the World, Part 1. *The "why" of evangelism.*

7. The Servant's Ministry in the World, Part 2. *The ways of evangelism.*

8. The Servant's Ministry in the World, Part 3. *Servant evangelism.*

9. The Servant's Ministry in the World, Part 4. *Relational evangelism.*

10. The Servant's Ministry in the Church. *Practical service in the family of God.*

11. More than a Disciple—a Servant, Part 1. *Scriptural servanthood.*

12. More than a Disciple—a Servant, Part 2. *Scriptural servanthood.*

13. More than a Disciple—a Servant, Part 3. *Servant leadership.*

14. The Servant's Reward. *Earthly and eternal rewards.*

The Re-Encounter Weekend Retreat

The Re-Encounter Weekend Retreat continues to prepare the disciple of Jesus to become *more than a disciple.* He or she develops into a sanctified servant of Jesus and a servant leader of his or her own life group.

At the Re-Encounter, attitudes and vision are focused directly on God. Faith, temptations, and spiritual warfare are discussed. Brokenness, transparency and the dynamics of dying to self become clear. The spiritual health and vitality of servant leaders are dealt with by the Holy Spirit's power. The heart issues of true servants of Jesus are explored and cleansed by the ongoing sanctification of God's Word and his Spirit.

Only those who have attended the Encounter and completed the follower's course, the disciple's course, *and* the servant's course are invited to the Re-Encounter Weekend Retreat.

The Re-Encounter Weekend

A retreat designed to help the emerging servant leaders
deal with the temptations and issues of leading
a life group and discipling others.
There are eleven sessions at the Re-Encounter Weekend

1. The Responsibility of a Christian Before the World
2. The Things Jesus Did in Me
3. Restoring Our Emotions
4. The Things Jesus Did for Me: The Cross
5. The Spiritual Kingdom and the Armor of God
6. How to Identify Bondages
7. How to Conquer Every Area of Our Lives and the Things Jesus Can Do Through Us
8. The Priesthood Family
9. The Consecration of a Leader
10. Excellence and Ethics of a Leader. Purity and holiness
11. The Anointing of the Holy Spirit

The Disciple-Maker's Course

Three months of one-and-a-half-hour sessions

The disciple-maker's course completes the year-long training from believer to dedicated disciple-maker. In this advanced course, the servant of Jesus moves into the area of making disciples as our Lord commanded. This is where the multiplication happens.

These classes include training in Christian maturity, the Holy Spirit, fruitfulness, and disciple-making. Additional training will be given in the areas of spiritual gifts, contagious Christianity, harvesting of souls, and the mature Christian's life as well as his or her walk with God.

The disciple-maker continues serving his or her life group and begins mentoring the people of the group. Assignments for this step last for three months. This quarter of training includes reading and growing their life group to ten or more. The disciple-maker must actively share his or her faith, maintain his or her Bible memorization, and complete a fourth journey through the New Testament. He or she should persuade his or her life group members to attend the Encounters so they may start down their own path of the Master's Plan courses.

The devoted disciple-maker continues the multiplication process with his or her life group. In the process, he or she demonstrates faithfulness, fruitfulness, and commitment to the vision of multiplication. As the group grows and souls are saved, reproduction is plainly seen.

The disciple-maker will be invited into his or her leader's lead group. This small group of no more than twelve is closed in the sense that it is not offered to everyone. Lead groups are for faithful, fruitful servant leaders who have completed all the above training. These groups meet weekly for mutual love, encouragement, training, prayer, accountability, and strategizing on how to reach more people for Jesus.

Eventually, each servant leader sees the people in his or her life group move through the believer, follower, disciple, servant, and disciple-maker courses. These people open their own life groups. At that point, the disciple-maker forms his or her own lead group, which may someday have as many as twelve faithful leaders.

There are ten sessions in the disciple-maker's course, which will be discussed in chapter 6. Each of these sessions covers the principles of disciple-making. In this course, the student will study sixty principles of successful discipling. Each principle contains the scriptural foundation for and the practical application of the principle in the life of the disciple and the disciple-maker. This course is designed to give the disciple-maker-in-training the insights and concepts necessary to be a successful, competent discipler. He or she will know how to actually work with new Christians and become not just a disciple of our Lord Jesus, but eventually also a disciple-maker. This is the fourth and final quarter of the Master's Plan year-long school for leaders.

Jesus modeled discipling in this way. He poured his life into twelve faithful, fruitful men and then empowered them to continue discipling others, just as he had discipled them. They knew how to do it because he had faithfully done it for them. After he gave the Great Commission, he didn't need to give them twenty more chapters on how to make disciples—he had modeled it for them for three years. He said, "As the Father has sent Me, I also send you" (John 20:21).

They were *sent*, and they *went*, and they did exactly what he had told them to do. They made disciples of Jesus who would make more disciples of Jesus. I cannot stress this enough. Our God is a God of multiplication. It is his will and his command that we go and multiply disciples of Jesus who will become multiplying disciple-makers.

The apostle Paul understood the basic strategy and plan of his Master. The Bible records that when he wanted to establish the new disciples in Ephesus, he found twelve men and poured his life into them for a concentrated time, about two years.[2] The end result of this focused attention on these key men was that the entire subcontinent of Asia Minor heard the Word of God regarding Christ's plan of salvation in just a couple of years. The Master's Plan works! Paul wrote these words to his young pastor-disciple: "The things which *you* have heard from *me* in the presence of many witnesses, entrust these to *faithful men* who will be able to teach *others* also" (2 Tim. 2:2, emphasis added).

Four "spiritual generations" can be found in that one verse:

- First generation = Paul, the founding leader who wrote this verse. Paul is the "me."
- Second generation = Timothy, the young pastor whom Paul wrote this verse to. Timothy is the "you" in this verse.
- Third generation = "faithful men."
- Fourth generation = "others."

This is our mandate, our model, and the Master's Plan.

six

Basic Principles of Disciple-Making

✦ The Master's Plan fourth-quarter curriculum is called the disciple-maker's course. This material covers sixty principles of disciple-making in over two hundred pages. These principles of discipling others are applicable to any model of disciple-making, not just the Master's Plan.

In this chapter we will not attempt to cover all sixty of those issues. This material is available on request from the author. For our purposes, we'll briefly cover a few basic principles that help us think about making multiplying disciples of Jesus.

Here is a very short list of the driving values of making Christlike disciples of Jesus:

1. *Jesus is the model of all biblical disciple-making.* We must study Jesus and his methodology. We must not only be faithful to his teachings and moral example—we must be true to his tactics. Jesus did it best. He is the genius of the universe. His model will forever remain the absolute best; it is impossible to improve on his great prototype.

2. *The Great Commission, Matthew 28:18-20, is God's nonoptional command for every Christian.* We are commanded to make Christlike disciples of every nation, who, in turn, do *all* that Jesus commanded us to do. That, of course, includes making more Christlike disciples.

3. *Like begets like.* Whatever we are, we will reproduce. We indeed teach and preach what we know, but we reproduce what we are. If I want to make Christlike disciples of Jesus, then I must become a Christlike disciple of Jesus myself. Personal purity and holiness are nonnegotiable in discipling others.

4. *To make Christlike disciples will demand a lot of time invested in baby Christians.* You cannot do this quickly and easily. It takes massive amounts of energy, money, and focused effort to raise a child. Raising spiritual children to become like Jesus requires no less effort. Discipling is spiritual parenting. It is incredibly time-intensive. Still, nothing we do is more important than making disciples of Jesus.

5. *Jesus said that he would build his church. He gave us the job of making disciples.* Our job is not to build the church. That's his job. Our job is to make disciples of the new converts he gives us. If we grow too busy trying to do Jesus' job of building the church that we have no time or energy left to invest in making his disciples, we are disobedient to his commands.

6. *You cannot truly disciple hundreds or even dozens of people at the same time.* You can preach or teach to thousands at once. You can pray over multitudes and lead them in joyous worship, yet you cannot truly mentor, coach, spiritually parent, or disciple more than a few people at a time. Jesus preached to thousands for days at a time. He healed all who came to him. He loved everybody, but he truly discipled only twelve men. A wise discipler will not try to disciple

or personally coach more people than the perfect, all-powerful Son of God.

7. *Spend more time with fewer people.* This is exactly what Jesus and Paul did. The majority of Jesus' ministry time was spent investing in his twelve disciples.

8. *Seek God for a long time. Fervently and passionately search for his hand-picked disciples to invest your life in.* Again, we love everybody, we preach to as many as possible, we even minister to as many as we can, but we pour our lives and spend the majority of our time with the disciples whom the Lord has called us to disciple. Jesus, the holy, all-wise Son of God, spent all night praying over who he should invite into his inner circle of twelve disciples.[1]

9. *All godly discipling is rooted in relationships and prayer.* Everything we do in making disciples of Jesus must be grounded in intense, fervent, passionate, persistent daily prayer, both for and with our disciples. As we pray for our disciples daily, it builds within us a great compassion for them. There is no discipling without love and committed relationships. The disciples all knew they were tremendously loved by Jesus!

10. *Christlike discipling consists of modeling. You imitate me, as I imitate Christ.*[2] This must not be only Paul's most famous operating motto, it has to become our own as well. Few Christians today feel comfortable saying those biblical words to their disciples, but that is exactly what God has called us to do. We are to be Christlike examples to our disciples in everything. (See 1 Timothy 4:12; Titus 2:7; 1 Peter 5:3).

11. *We don't make disciples of us—we make disciples of Jesus.* Properly speaking, they are never *our* disciples—they are his. They are, however, our *spiritual sons and daughters* in the faith. More than a few times in Scripture, Paul referred to his disciples as his spiritual children. In the Word they were also called Paul's disciples. But Paul never forgot that they were first and foremost Jesus' disciples. Our spiritual children are our responsibility and joy.

12. *Only Jesus can give a person new life and salvation.* He alone can convict, save, forgive, cleanse, and make new believers. He does this through us as we intercede for souls. We must faithfully live and witness to others through the power of the Holy Spirit. Jesus is the One who can make new believers. *Once they become believers, it is our job to make disciples of Jesus out of them.*

13. *The best definition of discipling* that we have run across was given to the Christian world by Allen Hadidian: "Discipling others is the process by which a Christian with a life worth emulating commits himself/herself for an extended period of time to a few individuals who have been won to Christ, the purpose being to aid and guide their growth to maturity and equip them to reproduce themselves in a third spiritual generation."[3]

14. *Content + context = discipling.* We must have both. One will never be enough. *Content* is information and facts. *Content* is Bible knowledge and theology. Content is taught. We need godly content to make a disciple of Jesus. It is essential, but it is not enough.

Context is *life to life.* It is modeling, coaching, mentoring, correcting, listening, observing, questioning, and discipling. It is spending life together and living life out together. *Context* is *caught.* We need Christlike context to truly disciple others.

15. *Love and minister to all, but invest your limited time only in discipling F.A.T. people.*

16. *There is no discipleship without discipline.* Both the discipler and the disciple will need to demonstrate godly discipline to follow through on this most important investment, time.

17. *Discipling is never urgent, but it is both extremely and eternally important.* Too often our lives are so consumed with the pressing, *urgent* demands of the day that we never get around to the most important things.

18. *Multiplication is the only principle that will get the job done and reach the world.* Addition is good, but multiplication is God's plan to reach the billions who are going to hell. Our God is a God of multiplication; he commanded us to be fruitful and *multiply.*

19. *Everybody needs a discipler, and everybody needs to be discipling a disciple.* Who is discipling you? Who are you discipling? Everybody needs a "Paul," a spiritual elder in his or her life. We all need someone who will hold us accountable, encourage us, pray for us, and disciple us. Every Christian also needs a "Timothy" in his or her life. Timothys are our little brothers or younger sisters in the Lord. We all need someone in whom we are investing time, prayer, love, and encouragement and whom we coach and mentor for Jesus.

20. *No one can become Christlike by himself or herself.* John Wesley famously declared, "There is no holiness without social holiness."[4] Social holiness to Wesley meant small-group accountability, prayer, and encouragement. We really do need each other in order to be like Jesus. No one becomes like Jesus all alone!

21. *There are basic components to making a Christlike disciple of Jesus.* We need a number of components to see a true life transformation. We need—

- **Salvation**—We need to be saved and to work with people who have truly been converted. It is difficult to disciple a demon or a demon-influenced person.

- **Sanctification**—It will take sanctification of both the discipler and the disciple to make more Christlike disciples.

- **Information**—this is content. This is curriculum. Information is the Bible. It is good theology. It is Romans 8 and the Sermon on the Mount. It is good, Christian books, CDs, conferences, speakers, preaching, and teaching. Information is essential, but information alone does not create a transformed life. Information all by itself can never make a Christlike disciple of Jesus who multiplies and makes more Christlike disciples.

- **Formation**—Formation is discipling, coaching, mentoring, and spiritual parenting. It is true *context*. It is personal, intimate, and time-consuming. It is patiently listening to the disciple and asking probing questions. It is praying together and implementing accountability. It is simultaneously doing life. It is one-on-one. It is spiritual guardianship. It is what Jesus did with the Twelve. Formation insures that our *information* is truly being understood, grasped, and applied in the life of our disciple. Formation involves assignments and follow-up on spiritual projects. It is personal tutoring in practical holiness. Formation is what happens when a disciple of Jesus honestly has a Christlike spiritual director who invests time and attention in him or her on a regular, long-term basis.

- **Conformation**—Everything we do must be aimed toward conforming to the image of Christ. Our goal is to help ourselves and our disciples become conformed to Christ in every area of our lives. Jesus is our Model, our Example, our First Love, our Hero, and our Goal. Becoming like Jesus must be the passion of our lives. Christlikeness = holiness.

Salvation + Sanctification + Information + Formation + Conformation = *Transformation*

Our disciples need salvation, sanctification, information, formation, and conformation to experience the lasting transformation that leads to spiritual multiplication. Only then can the Father bring true *multiplication*! Why would he really want to multiply anything, be it a ministry or a life, if it does not result in Christlike disciples of Jesus? Why would God want to multiply carnality or selfishness? These are just a few basic principles of Christian disciple-making.

 seven

The Two Types of Small Groups in the Master's Plan

✦ There are two types of groups in the Master's Plan. Both are essential. John Wesley developed an interlocking system of small groups to aid believers in their journey of holiness. The Master's Plan also incorporates two essential types of small groups.

1. The open, evangelistic life group.
2. The closed, select group of leaders.

Each of these groups meets weekly and is distinct in its function and purpose.

The Open, Evangelistic Life Group

The open, evangelistic life group is led by a trained, discipled leader who continues to be discipled and coached by his or her discipler. It may be a same-sex group, mixed-gender group, or couples group. Many churches find same-sex groups work best. Ideally they consist of several leaders:

- A leader who is being discipled and led by someone and who is under the authority and coaching of a Christlike leader.
- A coleader—an assistant or "Timothy," that is, someone in training to be a leader himself or herself who is being discipled by the small-group leader.
- A host or hostess if you are meeting in someone's home. Refreshments may or may not be provided.

The size of these groups can be anywhere from three to twenty-five people. Experience has shown us that in any group with over eight members, there will typically be some who will not get a chance to share during a regular meeting. Many groups like to split once they grow to six and beyond.

These life groups can meet anywhere. A home, church, restaurant or coffee shop, business conference room or office—even the great outdoors makes a good place to gather. What's crucial is consistency in the time and place. Don't move the group around a lot. It's confusing. People must know when and where they are meeting.

The best groups usually meet for no more than an hour. If you go much longer, people will soon stop attending. It's better to quit while they want more. Linger beyond the recommended period, and people might stay away. As a point of integrity, end on time. If people hang around later to visit— great. But have a regular, you-can-count-on-it dismissal time.

Everyone is welcome to come to these open evangelistic life groups. They are called *evangelistic* groups because the ultimate purpose of these gatherings is *not* Bible study, fellowship, accountability, worship, or just having fun together. Now all these elements will happen in the life of these open meetings, but that is not their primary goal. The winning of souls is their objective. In these life groups, prayer by name for lost people is consistently made. The gospel is shared with any who attend and do not know Christ.

Bible studies are great. We all love them, but most Christians don't need yet another Bible study. They need to apply the biblical information they've already received. There is a place for fellowship groups, accountability groups, service groups, affinity groups, worship groups, and groups focusing on a common ministry, but sadly, these groups typically do not multiply. They may add, but they rarely multiply. Many healthy Master's Plan groups multiply into two or more groups every sixth months.

It's extremely common in our Evangelical churches to have Sunday School classes that provide wonderful Bible studies, fellowship, and prayer, but they never grow much. I know of great Bible study groups that have met together for over twenty years and have not grown by one person in that entire time. There's a place for these kinds of nongrowth groups—just not in the Master's Plan. They are not helpful or central to actually doing the Master's Plan. God called us to be fruitful and multiply. That can happen through the open, evangelistic life groups found in the Master's Plan.

The focus of these open groups is pure, simple evangelism. We want to see people saved by Jesus Christ. In and through these groups, we do. We want to plug new Christians into these groups and see them flourish, immediately growing into soul-winning multipliers.

To do what these life groups are designed to accomplish, follow a simple hour-long format. Here is what a typical Master's Plan, open, evangelistic life group agenda looks like:

- **Warm-up**—thirty minutes. Before the group meets, the leader and their Timothy (leader in training), meet for a half hour of fervent prayer for the group that is about to meet. Each individual who is a part of the group is prayed over, as is the agenda for that meeting. The leaders can pray the Prayer of Three.
- **Welcome** and gathering in—five minutes.
- **Worship** and brief prayer—five minutes or less.

- **Word**—twenty minutes. This can be a brief devotional by the leader based on last Sunday's message. Bibles are open for this part of the meeting, but primarily the purpose here is not another Bible study. If someone shows up who doesn't know the Lord, the leader uses this time to give a simple explanation of the gospel and salvation (salvation plans such as the Roman Road to Salvation or the Four Spiritual Laws are both easy to understand and readily available on the Internet). An opportunity is given for all to pray the prayer of repentance. Only at the conclusion of this prayer does the Bible study take place. People get saved in these brief meetings. Praise the Lord!

- **Word of Testimony**—ten minutes. See Revelation 12:11. The group briefly shares what they are doing about what they have learned in God's Word. This can include their actions in obedient response to what God spoke to them from last Sunday's message or from their own personal devotions. Questions we love to address are "What is God teaching you?" and "What are you doing about it?"

- **Work**—ten minutes. Break into groups of three and pray for each other. The first real work in spiritual matters is always *prayer.* We can do a lot of work afterward, but we dare not try any work, for God or others, without putting the hard work of prayer first. Prayer is work! Don't waste time sharing prayer requests—this can eat up all the time you have allotted for prayer. Each person who feels comfortable praying aloud goes ahead and prays. They share their concerns in prayer with God, and the others agree in prayer.

- **Warfare**—ten minutes. While still in those groups of three, the small group prays for lost people using the highly effective tool of the Prayer of Three. Here is how it works:
  - A small group of three people pray for each other's short list of three names of lost people. This gives us a total of nine names that the triad is praying for in a consistent, passionate, fervent manner.
  - These same three prayer partners continue to *pray daily* for at least three minutes for three months for the total list of nine people. Each time the open, evangelistic life group meets, the same three people get into a tight circle and continue praying for those same nine.
  - For the last three weeks of prayer, the threesome should also fast. After three months of daily personal intercession for those nine people and weekly small-group prayer in their prayer of three, each individual commits to share Christ with the three people whom the threesome have prayed for. Next they invite them to an evangelistic event. The small group of three prayer warriors holds each other accountable in following through on this commitment. They continue praying and fasting as they personally invite their three to Jesus or to an evangelistic event.
  - God answers prayer. People who have been fervently prayed over for three months get saved! They become a part of the life group, and the life group begins to pray for their short list of three names. The multiplication continues. Those who

don't get saved are repeated in the Prayer of Three cycle until they come to faith in Christ. Without a question, the single most powerful and effective thing that happens in these open, evangelistic life groups is the Prayer of Three. Not coincidentally, this is the one component that many Christians struggle with the most. It is no wonder since this is what Satan fears the most in our groups or at home. Prayer terrifies the devil. Make no mistake—when you pray fervently, the enemy will fight. He knows it is the key to ruining his wicked plans. Never quit praying the Prayer of Three.

- **Wrap-up.** The leader and his or her Timothy meet to do a *postgame analysis* of how the meeting went. Prayer is offered for each person who attended and those who couldn't make it that time. Plans are laid for next week's meeting.

- **Witness.** This is what God has called each of us to be and do. All week long, each member prays while looking for opportunities to share Christ with lost people. Later on it's exciting to share with the group how God used each person to witness, to speak of his gospel to unsaved people.

The Closed, Select Group of Leaders

The closed, select group of leaders is the second type of small group that is essential to the Master's Plan. They also meet weekly, but their focus on membership, their characteristic, and their purpose are greatly different from the open, evangelistic life group.

This group is closed. It is not advertised in the church bulletin. It is by invitation only. It is made up of leaders of life groups that have proven to be F.A.T. people:

F—Faithful

A—Available

T—Teachable

These are life group leaders who have—

- Been through the Encounter Weekend Retreat.
- Completed the year-long curriculum of courses and classes.
- Faithfully been a part of someone else's open life group.
- Successfully started their own open, evangelistic life group.
- Faithfully continue to lead their open, evangelistic life group.
- Led others to Christ—they are fruitful!
- Grown in personal purity, holiness, and Christlikeness.
- Proven faithful to the vision and mission of the Master's Plan.
- Been prayed over by the leader. God has led the leader to personally invite them into this closed group of leaders. These closed groups can be called by any name you desire. Some churches call them lead groups, closed cell groups, the 12, G12 groups, leader's groups, accountability groups, or Master's Plan groups.

Typically, these Master's Plan groups of leaders meet weekly for an hour and a half to two hours or more. They consist of one leader and their disciples, who are all leaders of life groups. It is highly recommended that these groups be no larger than one leader and twelve disciples as Jesus focused his primary ministry on no more than twelve disciples. Supervisory experts and experience has taught that it's difficult for a person to adequately coach more than twelve individuals at a time.

Some leaders start their group of leaders with just one or two, adding more over time as God gives them direction and new F.A.T. leaders. In the Appendix of this book is a list of recommended qualities a leader should demonstrate before being invited into a lead group.

Take your time in developing this crucial group of leaders and multipliers. Some pastors take years to complete their twelve. The worst mistake you can make is just to go out and grab twelve folks from your church and try to get them to grow into F.A.T. leaders of the Master's Plan. Do this and you may end up wanting to fire most of them. You will fail to multiply.

The members of this group become the leader's spiritual sons or daughters. They are the primary persons who continue the process of dynamic multiplication. Let it be the goal and dream of each member of the lead group to someday have his or her own group of twelve disciples.

It is highly recommended that these closed groups be made up of people of the same gender. A men's group should be led by a man with no more than twelve men, just as a ladies' group should be made up of a female leader with no more than twelve women. They meet weekly to—

- Hear from the leader's heart a word that they have received from the Lord for the small group of leaders.
- Encourage the leader and be encouraged by the leader.
- Pray for each other and their leader.

- Do real spiritual warfare together.
- Share what God is teaching them in their own personal devotions.
- Do the Prayer of Three for lost people.
- Be further trained by the leader and one another.
- Engage in open, honest, humble accountability and confession.
- Share what is going on in their life groups and with their disciples.
- Be involved in the mutual training and in the best practices of discipling real, messy, living, breathing disciples.
- Share life together.
- Share wisdom from the Word with each other.
- Bear one another's burdens as Jesus commanded us to in Galatians 6:2.
- Work on problems or challenges that no one discipler can handle on his or her own.
- Strategize how to reach more lost people and organize evangelistic events.

These closed groups of leaders become very close. True *koinonia* fellowship happens as trust, transparency, vulnerability, encouragement, and prayer draw the group tighter and tighter. *Agapē* love reigns in these powerful meetings.

The leader models what his or her lead group is aiming for by his or her Christlike compassion, sanctified servanthood, and gracious leadership. In his or her humble and broken selflessness, the leader supports and encourages the disciples God has given him or her. Together the group grows in Christlikeness and obedience. Together they work, plan, pray, and strive together to see the Great Commission accomplished through their lives and the lives of their disciples.

Some leaders of disciples meet weekly with each of their disciples for personal accountability, coaching, and mentoring in Christlike grace and practical, personal holiness. God bonds the discipler and his or her disciples together in great love and loyalty to one another. The *one anothers* of the New Testament—there are over forty of them[1]—can be lived out in this kind of intentional community of faithful, disciple-making believers.

Eventually, the leader's closed group of faithful leaders multiplies. Each of those twelve leaders someday, by God's grace and power, has his or her own group of multiplying disciples. They, of course, will lead their own life groups.

The multiplication is only beginning. May it continue until our Lord Jesus Christ returns in glory!

 eight

The Journey of "Joe Unbeliever" to "Joe Disciple-Maker"

↩ It might be helpful to get an overview of how the Master's Plan works in the life of a single person who is won to Christ and discipled in this dynamic model. Let's call this fictional person "Joe Unbeliever." We'll follow Joe through the various stages of his Christian life and growth as a new believer in the Master's Plan. For the sake of our story, we will assume Joe is both compliant and cooperative with his disciplers. He eagerly follows through on what he is challenged to do as he learns to walk with God.

Joe is a nice guy. He loves his family and is a decent human being. He is a good provider and cares about his two kids. He is thirty-five and in fairly good shape, but is an unbeliever. He has no interest in God, church, or spiritual matters. However, God blessed Joe because he happened to have a friend named Chris Christian. Joe didn't know it, but through prayer, Jesus Christ and Chris have been discussing him for some time.

Chris and Joe have been acquaintances for a long time. Both work together at the plant and share a common interest in the Los Angeles Lakers. They even watch a game or two on television during the playoffs. They genuinely like each other. If the truth be told, they trust each other. Joe is impressed with Chris's work ethic and the fact that he honestly cares about others. Chris has once or twice tried to engage Joe in a spiritual conversation, but Joe quickly changed the subject. He really isn't all that interested in "spiritual stuff."

Chris attends a church that is beginning to implement the Master's Plan model of disciple-making. He accepted the pastor's invitation and attended his first Encounter Weekend Retreat. It blew him away. God did a real number on his heart. Chris got personal issues with God squared away and took part in the classes the church offered for those who had attended the Encounter. He learned to put his faith to work in his everyday life. Chris grew in Christlikeness and felt an increasing burden for the guys at work who didn't know Jesus.

Chris followed the encouragement of Pastor Bill and became a part of his open, evangelistic men's life group that meets for an hour on Thursday nights. He felt impressed by the sincerity, openness, and honesty of the life group.

Very shortly after Chris joined this life group of nine guys, the pastor challenged him to share with a couple of other guys in the group the names of three men Chris knew who needed to give their lives to Jesus. Chris immediately thought about Joe and shared his friend's name with the other two guys in his triad, Sam and Tom. All three of them, Chris, Tom, and Sam, submitted the names of three men they had contact with who needed Jesus.

They prayed over the nine men. Not only was Joe Unbeliever prayed for by Chris, but by two guys he had never met. They prayed for him each day, along with the other eight men whose names were on their short list. Every Thursday night in Pastor Bill's life group, toward the end of their hour together, Chris, Sam, and Tom huddled up to pray fervently for the salvation of Joe Unbeliever. Joe had no idea anyone prayed for him so passionately. He had no clue God was preparing to interrupt his life.

Chris and his two prayer buddies continued to pray the Prayer of Three for three months. The last few weeks, Chris fasted at lunchtime, praying specifically for the nine guys on their prayer list. Chris sensed that something was about to happen that would change Joe's eternity.

It did.

Joe's beautiful wife, Nancy, had an awful accident and hovered between life and death. The doctors gave little hope that they could save her. Joe felt desperate. He didn't know what to do as he paced the waiting room at the hospital. Was he about to lose his wife? And then, for some reason, he thought of Chris Christian. Chris believed in God and probably knew how to pray in an emergency. Feverishly, he entered Chris's number on his cell phone. Chris answered.

Joe couldn't help himself. His tears made long tracks down his cheeks, and his voice cracked as he told Joe what had happened. Chris promised he would rush over to the hospital. Joe begged him to pray. Chris replied that he was already praying.

Chris drove like a madman, praying for all he was worth: *O God—spare Joe's wife, Nancy! Please show Joe how great and gracious you are. Let him understand how you respond to prayer and that you care for him and his wife.* At several red lights, Chris quickly called Pastor Bill, Sam, and Tom, telling them to pray for Joe and Nancy. They all hit their knees.

Chris finally arrived at the hospital. The night grew ever-longer as they waited. They sipped the stale hospital coffee and paced together in the empty surgery waiting room. At last, Chris felt led to lay his hand on Joe's shoulder and pray out loud. Joe wept throughout both the prayer and the evening. After a long wait, the doctor came through the doors. He was not smiling.

Joe's heart sank.

The doctor explained how they had almost lost Nancy several times. Then he said, "It was incredible. When we thought it was all over—unexplainably, she began to rally. Her numbers moved toward a more normal range. She's now resting in the recovery room. Joe, you can see her in a little while, but keep it brief." The doctor then left.

Joe melted in Chris's arms, relieved beyond words. Chris and Joe hugged in a long embrace. Joe couldn't believe what he heard himself say next: "God heard your prayers, Chris."

Chris only nodded and said, "Thank you, God!"

Nancy slowly recovered and Joe Unbeliever was never the same. He had almost lost the most precious person in his life. When he needed a friend most, Chris had blown him away. He had not only come over, but had also spent that long night beside him in the hospital. Then Chris had prayed. Oh, no—Joe hadn't forgotten that. Joe didn't know much about either prayer or God, but he was convinced that God had heard Chris's heartfelt prayer that night.

Not long after that, Joe felt a strong urge to spend more time with Chris. Joe asked him questions about God, prayer, miracles, and what had really happened on that fateful night.

By this point, Chris, Sam, and Tom had been praying for Joe Unbeliever for over three months. They had even experimented with prayer and fasting. Countless times, Joe's name had been lifted to God in passionate intercession. They begged God for Joe's soul. They had even prayed for both Nancy's recovery and her salvation.

Joe approached Chris and told him that he had a lot of questions "about God and stuff." That day they shared lunch together. Joe indeed had a lot of questions. In the end, Chris told him about his small men's group who met on Thursdays and how they had been praying for him and Nancy. Joe could barely believe that strangers had cared enough to pray for him and his wife. He was incredibly grateful.

Almost as an afterthought, Chris invited Joe to that Thursday night's meeting. Joe agreed to go. Chris could hardly believe it—maybe there really was something to this whole prayer business! Chris called Pastor Bill, Sam, and Tom and told them the incredibly good news: Joe Unbeliever was coming to the open men's life group that Thursday night.

Pastor Bill called the six others in the small group and they all focused their prayers with fasting on Chris, Joe, and the Thursday night meeting. Sure enough, Joe kept his word, showing up with Chris at the meeting.

Pastor Bill and the other men welcomed Joe warmly. Joe Unbeliever could not believe how warm and friendly these guys were. Something was different about these men. Pastor Bill shared the gospel message in a simple, down-to-earth manner. Then he quietly asked if anyone there that evening wanted to know God personally, giving his life to Jesus in an act of repentance and surrender.

Joe found himself raising his hand.

The other guys were so excited they cheered and clapped him on the back. The pastor prayed a simple prayer. All the men, including Joe, repeated phrase by phrase the prayer out loud to God. Joe Unbeliever was changed for eternity. He was no longer "Joe Unbeliever." In a single moment of faith he became "Joe Believer"!

The other guys were thrilled for Joe. Joe wept joyously. He had never felt this way before. Unable to describe how he felt, he cried and laughed at the same time. His new brothers were also beside themselves with delight. Joe almost wondered if they had become drunk on something, but no booze had been offered at the meeting.

Joe Believer walked out of that life group a new man in Christ Jesus. He felt so grateful for Chris that he just had to thank him. "I can hardly believe it!" was all he could say.

On the way home, Chris encouraged him to tell Nancy what had happened. Joe was a little worried about that. He didn't know what Nancy would say, but he knew she was glad to be alive and that Chris had stayed with Joe all night at the hospital. She had been told how prayer had saved her life and that she believed.

Joe told Nancy that night. She didn't understand all that Joe was trying to say, but she hadn't seen her husband this crazy-happy for a long time. She figured she would wait and see if this new phase lasted very long.

The next day, Chris ran into Joe at work. They agreed to meet each day at lunch, checking in with each other on what was happening in their lives and praying a bit together. A few days later, Chris had a gift for Joe—a Bible. It even had Joe's name on the cover. Joe had never owned or even held a Bible before. Chris gave him some simple instructions about daily getting into God's Word. Chris promised to show him how to do that and try to answer any questions Joe may have on what he had read.

Joe asked if he could come to church with Chris that following Sunday. Chris smiled and said, "Sure." They agreed to meet for breakfast before church. Joe had never stepped inside a church. Later he began having some doubts about this whole church thing, but Chris and the other guys in the life group struck him as the real deal.

Sunday came and Joe Believer went with Chris to his church. The place was jumping with people. Joe was immediately impressed that all nine guys from the Thursday night group came up and shook his hand warmly. They seemed genuinely happy to see him. Every one of them knew his name. That amazed Joe. Of course he had no idea that he had been on their hearts and prayer lists for a long time.

The service went longer than Joe was prepared for, but the pastor's sermon turned out to be quite helpful. The music was exciting with a live band and everything. The people certainly looked happy. Everybody acted excited to meet him. Joe had to admit it—he was deeply impressed. Still, he wasn't sure what Nancy would think about all this.

Chris and Joe continued meeting daily. Chris taught Joe how to pray and how to get into the Bible daily. Each day they would share what they had recently learned from God's Word.

Joe enjoyed going to the Thursday night men's group. He found out that it was called a "life group." He thought it was a perfect name as it had become his lifeline in his early days as a Christian. These guys enjoyed sharing God's Word together, and they talked openly about what was going on in their lives. They kept themselves transparent and honest. Joe had never before found men who were so real.

Near the end of the first hour of his initial meeting as a new Christian, Joe was invited to share the names of three guys he knew who didn't really know God. The group said they wanted to pray for them. Joe could only think of a couple of names, but he was impressed that these guys would spend time praying for someone they didn't personally know. It felt a bit weird, but kind of in a good way.

Before the evening ended, a question crossed his mind: *I wonder if these guys prayed for me like this.* He asked Chris if they had prayed for him like those others whose names were on the list. Chris replied, "You have no idea how long and hard we prayed for you." Joe only laughed. These were nice guys and truly genuine, but a bit strange. Yet he liked them, and they surely seemed to like him.

A few weeks later on Sunday in church and later in the men's group, Pastor Bill mentioned they were going to hold a Men's Encounter Weekend Retreat in a month or so. Chris encouraged Joe Believer to go with him to the retreat. Joe wasn't too sure about leaving Nancy that long. She was still recovering, and there were the kids. Chris remained pretty insistent.

Nancy assured him she could handle the kids. In fact, she had noticed real changes for the better in Joe's behavior. He no longer cursed in front of the kids as he had before. When he had stopped drinking, she could hardly believe it. He was more gentle and tender with her. He still lost his temper some but was quick to apologize, even asking her forgiveness. He had *never* done that before. That men's group really was helping him grow into being a better husband and dad.

When Nancy heard about the men's-only retreat that was designed to bring them closer to God and be better husbands and fathers, she almost forced him out the door. This whole phase had lasted a lot longer than she had dared imagine. Maybe the whole deal was real after all.

Joe felt nervous about the upcoming Encounter Weekend Retreat, but he knew Chris and some of the other guys from the Thursday night group would be there. This made him feel a whole lot better. What Joe didn't know was that the men who were not able to go to the retreat were fasting and praying for Joe as he attended. They prayed that Joe would be set free and truly sanctified by God's Holy Spirit. Joe had no idea what he was about to encounter at the Encounter.

Chris and Joe attended the Saturday afternoon class called the "pre-Encounter." Joe's questions were answered and his fears were allayed by the humor, positive spirit, and joyful anticipation exhibited by everybody who had been to a previous Encounter. Guys got up and told everyone how God had really messed them over at the Encounter, but for the better. They were genuinely thrilled that Joe was about to encounter God at this upcoming retreat.

Joe was informed about what to bring and what not to bring to the retreat. He was instructed in the proper frame of mind that he needed as the event got closer. They talked about dealing with demons, being set free, getting sanctified, and being filled with the Holy Spirit. Joe wasn't entirely sure what he had gotten himself into by signing up, but he couldn't deny that God had already done quite a number on him, and after all, Chris was all for it. By now Chris had become his very best friend, and he didn't want to let him down. Besides, Chris had never yet steered him wrong.

Predictably, Chris and Joe sat together at the Encounter Retreat. From the very first moment, Joe felt something was powerfully different about this gathering of men. There was an air of excitement. People expected God to actually show up. They enjoyed a great meal, and then there was some pretty energetic singing. Again, everybody remained upbeat and positive.

Joe had never been around so many people like this before. "Real" was the only word that Joe could think of to describe them. They were honest about their own shortcomings, faults, and sins. These men didn't need to impress anybody; they truly cared about each other—and Joe.

The Encounter was literally something out of this world. Never had Joe experienced such a wide range of emotions among men who willingly expressed themselves and were vulnerable, real, and honest. They laughed, they cried, they sang, they prayed for each other, and they listened attentively. Joe finally had a vague concept of what Chris called the Holy Spirit. Joe felt a—a what? A presence? Yes. It was almost palpable.

In session after session, Joe felt the speaker was talking directly to him. During one of the breaks, he asked Chris if he had told the leaders about Joe's own sins and struggles. Chris simply smiled as he shook he head and said, "No way, man. That's the Holy Spirit nailing you."

After each session, everyone received an opportunity to personally pray, discussing anything spoken to him by God. Joe found himself opening up to Christ more than he had ever done in his entire life. God moved in this place. Joe had nothing to compare this to, not even Sunday morning services in church. This was focused, powerful, and intense, a true encounter with God.

The Lord had Joe's number on a whole lot of things.

When they talked about sexual purity, Joe thought about his online porn collection. That had to go. As they focused on forgiveness, Joe thought about his brother. The schmuck had really wronged him a long time ago. They had not spoken in years. Joe suddenly felt he needed—no, not just that—he *wanted* to forgive his brother. The men at his table helped him pray about this.

This was one intense weekend! Joe felt wrung out.

Next they talked about being set free from demonic forces that could harass or influence Christians. Joe struggled with lust, impurity, and especially anger. He asked the others to pray over him in these areas. The prayer was more powerful than he ever expected. Something happened! Almost instantly Joe felt something deep inside melt away. He felt lighter, happier. He felt free. He felt that with God's ongoing help, he could really walk in purity and holiness.

Then, the speaker talked about something called sanctification and the need to be filled with the Holy Spirit. As he listened, it became clear that Joe Believer needed that too. He stepped forward along with a whole room full of guys who stood weeping and solemnly declaring that they needed cleansing. They called out to be purified and filled with God's Holy Spirit.

Joe fell to his knees. The leaders laid their hands on his head, praying that he would be entirely sanctified and filled with God's Holy Spirit. It happened! Wow! Instantly, Joe knew God had kept his promise to give him the fullness of the Holy Spirit. That Saturday night, Joe Believer was transformed into "Joe Sanctified Believer."

In the last session of the Encounter, Pastor Bill challenged the men to commit themselves to a year's worth of classes designed to build on their Encounter experience, firmly establishing them in practical holiness. He challenged everyone to allow himself to be trained in becoming real followers of Jesus—and more.

The pastor promised that it was God's will that they become disciples of Jesus and someday even grow into disciple-makers. The leaders of the church committed themselves to help Joe and the other newly sanctified men become successful, effective disciple-makers for Jesus. By now, Joe felt more than willing to do anything for Jesus.

He rushed forward to sign up for the courses, only to be almost knocked over by a bunch of guys trying to beat him to it. Maybe they were afraid there was a limit to how many could sign up. It was unbelievable. Everybody wanted to get in on this!

Chris promised he would go through the entire year's classes with him. When Joe later realized Chris had already been through the whole year's training but was willing to do it again with him, he was amazed. Chris would help him through it all. Joe never knew there were friends like Chris Christian.

The classes began that following Monday night. There were homework assignments, and the classes ran for two hours. Joe wasn't used to intense learning, but he knew God was pleased with him. He liked pleasing God.

The first quarter was called the "follower's course." The class was instructed in how to not only read, but also study and obey God's Word. They learned how to pray more effectively and to victoriously handle temptations. Joe Believer grew increasingly challenged. God wanted him to be more than just a believer. He wanted him to be a faithful follower as well. In these ten classes, Joe dug deep into the Bible and discovered what our Lord said to him about being a true follower of Jesus. Joe longed to please God and become a faithful follower of Christ.

Joe Believer matured as he daily read God's Word and continued his frequent meetings with Chris. Joe found out that Chris was discipling him just as Jesus had discipled and coached his twelve disciples. By now, Joe had learned how all Christians are supposed to become disciples of Jesus and later evolve into being disciple-makers of other disciples for Jesus. Chris was patiently showing him how to do that by his own example.

Each week, Joe continued attending the follower's course as well as going to church on Sunday mornings. He honestly looked forward to the men's life group with Chris, Sam, Tom, and all the other great guys. They all prayed for Nancy and Joe's two kids to accept Christ.

By now, Nancy knew that whatever Joe had found was going to last. She also felt what he had stumbled onto was somehow real. She needed it too. It wasn't long after Joe learned in the follower's course how to lead somebody to Christ that he had the privilege of leading his sweet Nancy to Jesus. Joe sat hugging her, beside himself with joy.

Nancy struggled at first to fit into the church, but the ladies were so welcoming. Nancy went to the ladies' life group that met on Sunday mornings during Sunday School. As they received her into their hearts without hesitation, every defense she had faded away. They showered her with genuine affection, attentively listening to her every word. They showed that they really loved her. Before long, her heart melted with love for these precious ladies. Whatever they had was great, and it seemed contagious.

Joe knew Nancy was really hooked when she came home one day and announced that she had signed up to go to the upcoming Women's Encounter Weekend Retreat. He felt so excited. He and the Thursday night guys had prayed that Nancy would truly be sanctified at the retreat!

Joe Believer became Joe Follower during the follower's course, but he wanted more. He wanted to grow closer to Christ. Chris discipled him faithfully, and they talked things over. They confessed their sins and temptations to each other and then prayed together. What a friend he was!

Joe even found himself doing something he never could have imagined before: he witnessed to his neighbor Tony, who really needed Jesus. Tony was a piece of work. He was a loud-mouth, alcoholic, woman-chasing, carousing, drug-using pain in the neck! He was a mess, and nobody in the neighborhood wanted to even speak to him. He certainly needed Jesus. Joe couldn't understand how Tony's wife put up with him.

Tony was on Joe's short list for the prayer of three. For weeks the Thursday night guys prayed for Tony. Joe now saw how this prayer business really worked. Nancy had finally come to Christ—that was because of prayer!

Tony was regularly lifted to God by Pastor Bill, Sam, Tom, Chris, and Joe. Joe's faith steadily expanded until he knew that Tony who didn't have a prayer—suddenly did. *We're praying for him. He won't last long as a sinner under all this prayer!*

Joe also memorized Scripture each week. He had almost completed reading the whole New Testament. It was almost unbelievable!

One Monday night Joe had strep throat and was forced to miss the follower's course class. His throat felt bad, but he felt worse about missing the class on how to listen to Jesus. He didn't know how he was going to catch up. Later in the week, his faithful friend Chris showed up on his doorstep. He had the notes from the missed class and took the time to tutor Joe Follower. By the next Monday night, Joe was up to speed with the rest of the class.

Throughout the year's classes, Chris made sure Joe understood everything that was taught. Each week Chris quizzed Joe to make sure that he really got that week's lesson. If Joe ever had to miss a class, Chris caught him up before the next session. Joe never felt he was falling behind. Man, what a friend Chris proved to be! Joe wondered if he could ever be a friend like that to a younger brother in the faith. Chris promised that someday he would indeed be discipling somebody else.

Chris suggested that when Tony—Joe's foul-mouthed, hard-drinking, harder-living next-door neighbor—gave his heart to Jesus, then he, Joe, would become a discipler. Joe Follower would have the privilege of discipling Tony. Joe got a big laugh at that. "Yeah, right!" It was too much to believe. God was pretty great, but Tony was just too much.

After ten weeks of the follower's course, Joe joined the disciple's course. There was even more homework and memorization. Joe quickly found it took real work being a disciple of Jesus. He discovered that a disciple is a *disciplined learner* of someone else. Jesus was calling him closer into the inner circle of faith, obedience, and holiness. Joe wanted to be more intimate with Christ. The classes lined out in detail what it meant to be a devoted disciple of our Lord. This was a challenge. Thank God that with Chris's ongoing example and encouragement, Joe found himself becoming a truly committed disciple of the Son of God.

It wasn't always easy. Going to church every Sunday, attending the men's life group on Thursday night, attending the Monday night disciple's course, and meeting regularly with Chris for one-on-one discipling took some time-juggling, but he still couldn't let Chris down. Most of all, he refused to let Jesus down. Joe escalated in Christlikeness. God replaced most of the hobbies and questionable pastimes Joe used to delight in so much. Jesus was truly Joe's passion and first love.

Jesus helped Joe Disciple to become more and more like him. Joe now wept for Tony when he thought about him going to hell forever. He yearned to see him come to Jesus. Tony really needed salvation—bad.

Once or twice Joe tried to talk to Tony about the Lord, only to be cursed out in no uncertain terms. What once would have made Joe Unbeliever furious now only broke his heart—not for himself, but for Tony. Tony was lost. Joe sensed Tony's only chance of eternally missing hell and going to heaven was because God had heard Joe and his life group brothers' prayers. Thank God for the Thursday night guys and their fervent intercession for Tony. God had to somehow use Joe to share Jesus with him. Joe longed for the day when God would soften Tony's heart and allow him to speak to him about Christ.

Joe continued reading God's Word, memorizing verses, praying daily for Tony and others on the short list, and loving on Nancy. She was growing in Jesus as well. Joe couldn't believe the positive changes he saw in her. In some ways he barely recognized her. She was so much more patient with him and the kids. She had gotten softer in all the best ways. Daily she grew ever more compassionate, tender, and forgiving, and Joe knew how often he needed her forgiveness. Joe was amazed with Jesus' ability to change people like him and Nancy. He wondered if Pastor Bill and Chris were right about God's ability to transform even that vile Tony next door.

After ten weeks of the disciple's course, Joe had developed the disciplines of holy living and had learned how to be both a godly husband and father. Joe dimly reflected Jesus, his Master, in every dimension. At the conclusion of the disciple's course, Joe was encouraged to follow through with the rest of the courses. The next one was a ten-week course in servanthood called, oddly enough, the "servant's course." Joe was beginning to see a pattern here. In fact, Joe got it.

Week after week, Joe and the rest of the class learned from Scripture what it meant to be a sanctified, selfless, Christlike servant of God and of others. It was one thing to be a servant of Jesus—it was quite another thing to be "a slave of all," as Jesus commanded his disciples to become. Only God's ongoing sanctifying Holy Spirit could help Joe Disciple develop into Joe Servant of All. Oh, how Joe prayed for that to come! God again proved faithful. Joe changed in deep and profound ways.

Nancy noticed that Joe willingly served around the house more; in fact, he even asked what he could do to help her. She saw him patiently working with the kids, loving them with a tenderness that Joe Unbeliever had not been known for. She was impressed as she witnessed Joe becoming increasingly less selfish. Her mouth flew open when she heard Joe praying about someday figuring out a way to serve Tony next door. Joe even asked her if she would join with him in praying for that—that—Tony!

When Joe wondered if he would ever become a true sacrificial servant of others, he would think of how Chris faithfully served both Joe and Jesus. To Joe, Chris modeled Jesus over and over. Chris easily out-served everybody at work. Whenever Joe needed him, there stood Chris, a life-sized example of joyful servanthood.

Joe wanted to be more like Chris. He saw his mentor becoming closer to and more like Jesus each month. Amazingly, the guys in his group said that they saw Joe becoming more like Christ as well. That was kind of hard to believe, but these guys were known for their honesty.

Along the way, the Thursday night life group that Joe and Chris attended had grown. Some of the guys they had prayed for had come to Christ. Pastor Bill challenged Chris to head up his own Thursday night group with Joe. Sam and Tom instantly agreed to join with them. So the four of them started out with Chris as the leader. He asked Joe to become his "Timothy," his second-in-command. That meant that Joe was being trained to lead his own group someday.

At first, the new group struggled to expand. Pastor Bill continued coaching Chris privately, mentoring him so he wouldn't give up. The new group continued praying for Tony and the others on the short list. The meetings were good, but growth remained slow. Sometimes the other guys bailed out on a Thursday night and there would only be Chris and

Joe. That discouraged Joe, but Chris had been trained to use opportunities like this to pray for each other and really get after the Prayer of Three.

Tony was prayed for on levels he couldn't imagine. Slowly, one by one, the group grew. The guys invited men from the church who weren't involved in any other group. Many guys checked them out, and some even stuck. All who joined prayed for lost people and joined with Joe, who kept on praying for Tony—big, bad Tony.

Along the way, Joe completed his third quarter, the servant's course of the Master's Plan. He realized that he had been unbelievably challenged by God's Word. He embraced the lifestyle of a sacrificial and selfless servant of both his Lord Jesus and of others. True, he still had a ways to go, but he felt well on his way. Joe prayed for God to show him a place he could serve Tony and maybe crack open his hard heart a bit to let in the gospel.

Joe helped Chris with his life group. He attended worship services at the church and met with Chris for accountability and prayer each week. Soon he embarked on the last quarter of the Master's Plan courses—the disciple-maker's course.

In this course Joe studied sixty principles of disciple-making. He didn't feel up to this whole business of actually helping someone become a Christlike disciple. After all, he was still pretty new at this whole Christian deal. Chris assured him he would continue meeting with him. He would be there to coach him into becoming an effective disciple-maker.

Chris also reminded him how this was God's will for Joe's life. The living God would greatly help Joe in doing his will. Joe even quoted himself a verse he had memorized: "I can do all things through [Christ] who strengthens me" (Philippians 4:13). Joe reasoned that "all things" must also include discipling somebody else.

Through the training he had received, Joe now felt impressed to meet regularly with each of his two children, Joe Jr., who was eight years of age, and little Sally, who only just turned five. He set up a weekly appointment with each of them. This became a time he enjoyed. He showed his love for them, encouraged them, answered questions, listened to them, and prayed with them. Who knew kids had so much on their minds?

Chris had coached Joe in discipling. This helped Joe immensely. For the first time, Joe was actively and intentionally discipling his own children to follow Jesus. Best of all, after a while he had the privilege of leading both of them to Christ. Joe and Nancy were ecstatic.

The disciple-maker's course continued. Joe felt impressed all the way through the journey. He had become a believer, a follower, a disciple, a servant, and now he was studying to become a disciple-maker of Jesus, and Chris had faithfully walked every step beside him. He was *still* Joe's model in disciple-making.

Chris listened for hours to Joe's questions and concerns. There had been questions about the Bible, questions about marriage, questions about raising kids to follow Jesus, and so many more that even Joe lost track. Chris patiently discipled Joe into becoming an intentional maker of disciples of Jesus.

A while later, the class was invited to attend a Re-Encounter Weekend Retreat. Joe went expecting to have a great time in the Lord. He was not disappointed. The Holy

Spirit continued to drill deep into Joe's heart. Attitudes and issues were addressed and confronted that rocked Joe to his core. God sanctified him at levels and layers Joe didn't know he had. The Lord was preparing Joe to become a disciple-maker and leader of his own life group.

Then came the challenge from Pastor Bill. He told the class of disciple-makers it was time to start their *own* open, evangelistic life group. Joe was far from excited about the prospect, but there sat Chris right beside him—Chris, who had promised he would not let Joe fail.

Chris reminded Joe how he had witnessed the life group structure for almost a year. In fact, he told Joe he would help him out by giving up a few guys from his own life group to assist him. He assured him that he would continue to coach him and be there anytime he was needed.

By this time, Chris had been invited into Pastor Bill's lead group. The pastor and Chris knew that Joe was ready to lead his own life group. After much prayer and more coaching, Joe formed his own life group. It was less than a year since he had walked into his first life group.

Joe Disciple-Maker was making disciples for Jesus!

Joe's new group was conducted just as Joe had witnessed Pastor Bill and Chris running their life groups. Chris attended the first few months of Joe's life group, giving both moral and prayer support. Joe and the three other guys given to him from Chris's group met at a coffee shop on Friday mornings before work. Joe could hardly believe God was using him, but he was.

Just as in the life groups Joe had participated in, Joe led his new group into the familiar component of the powerful Prayer of Three. Of course, the life group prayed for Tony.

A few months later, Joe graduated from the disciple-maker's course. He faithfully met with his kids, Joe Jr. and Sally, each week to listen his way into their hearts, pointing them to Jesus. He patiently instructed them how to listen to Jesus. He felt amazed at what they reported the Lord was teaching them. Nancy had her own time with each of the kids every week. Both Nancy and Joe were thrilled and almost shocked at how fast their kids were growing in the Lord.

Joe also met weekly with Chris for one-on-one discipling and coaching. Chris helped him understand just how to handle different situations that came up in his life group. Together they prayed for Joe's guys and for the next meeting of his life group. They all continued praying for Tony. It wasn't long before Joe Disciple-Maker was invited into Chris's new lead group for life group leaders. Joe was a leader. He was a disciple-maker.

This new group added whole new levels of encouragement, prayer, accountability, and brotherhood; so much so that Joe actively searched for practical ways he could show a little love to Tony. Weekly he pulled Tony's trash bins in from the street after the garbage men had passed through. Joe amazed Tony by mowing his lawn for him once in a while after doing his own.

Tony appeared sincerely touched by his efforts, but failed to understand Joe. One day Tony came right out and asked, "Why do you do what you do? Why do you care about me?"

Joe just replied, "I want to be a better neighbor."

Tony simply shook his head in disbelief.

Joe once barbequed up some particularly tasty steaks. Tony remarked over the fence that they sure smelled good. Joe instantly invited Tony to come over and join them for dinner. He was either too stunned or too hungry to say no. He had not always treated Joe with respect. That night both men felt surprised to be sitting in Joe's backyard sharing a great dinner. God was there, too, softening Tony's heart.

When Tony had to leave on a business trip that extended into a vacation, Joe offered to mow his lawn, take in the mail, feed his pets, and keep a close eye on his place. Tony gladly took Joe up on the offer.

Easter rolled around, and the church was sponsoring a special musical drama, including a presentation of the gospel and an opportunity for people to accept Christ. As Joe continued to pray for Tony, he felt impressed to invite him and his family to join them for the Easter musical. To Joe's utter surprise, Tony said, "Okay—sounds good to me. We've never been to a church. Maybe it's about time."

Leading up to the big day of the drama presentation, Joe and all his guys, including his own discipler, Chris, fervently prayed and fasted for Tony and his family. Joe hardly slept the night before the musical. What was God up to?

Joe was actually surprised that Tony did not back out at the last minute. He and his wife and three kids accompanied Joe and his family to the presentation. Joe could tell that Tony was very uncomfortable walking up to the church building. He made a nervous remark about lightning striking the place because he was setting his sinful feet in a holy church.

Tony made it inside the sanctuary without being divinely incinerated. The musical drama began. Joe scarcely heard the microphoned singers as he sat passionately pleading with Jesus to do something in Tony's heart. Joe kept his eyes politely open so as not to seem too wild and weird for Tony, but oh, how he prayed! Could this be Tony's moment?

When the presentation was almost over, Joe stole a glance at big, bad Tony—and saw a tear coursing down the tough guy's cheek. Somehow Joe knew that before long he would be discipling Tony in his new walk with Jesus, just as Chris had done so faithfully with him.

In a little over a year, Joe Unbeliever had transformed into Joe the productive disciple-maker!

 nine

The Next Steps

✧ What steps should a pastor take if he or she feels led to further look into the Master's Plan? What are the suggested steps to get going in this powerful, multiplying model? The following is a laundry list other pastors and leaders found helpful in getting started in this vision.

1. **Study and learn** all you can about the Master's Plan. (See the Resources Consulted section at the end of the book.)
   - Read Rocky Malloy's book *The Jesus System Groups of 12.*
   - Read Cesar Castellanos' books. Recognize that Cesar Castellanos is a charismatic. You may disagree with his emphasis on tongues and other charismatic manifestations. If reading charismatic Christian authors bothers you or upsets your faith, skip these.
   - Read Joel Comiskey's books.
   - Look over the materials that various Nazarene pastors and others are developing for the Master's Plan. You may want to create your own or borrow heavily. You are welcome to use the Master's Plan our denomination is presenting through Nazarene Publishing House and Sunday School and Discipleship Ministries International. You can adapt it as God leads you.
   - If you can, travel to Cali, Colombia, to see for yourself what God is doing with this model. Attend the

church's annual conference and great rallies. Be prepared to be spoiled against doing church the "normal" way for the rest of your life. You have been warned. You will be forever changed!

- Take your time. Many pastors study this model for a year or two before they commit to it. It is a huge step and a lot of work. At Anaheim First Church of the Nazarene, we spent an entire year studying it before implementing this model. We probably should have taken longer.

- Recognize that this is a huge commitment to change. In many ways there is no turning back once you get going. Most of your people won't want to turn back. Transition is never easy. As someone once said, "Only babies like to be changed, though many of them fuss, cry, and scream *while* you're changing them."

2. **Attend a Nazarene Pastor's and Leader's Training Day on the Master's Plan.** This is offered at Nazarene churches across North America. Go to a Nazarene Encounter Weekend Retreat as a participant, *not* a critical analyst. Let God do whatever he wants to in your heart. Experience it firsthand. Prepare to be challenged, convicted, and changed. Don't try to pull off an Encounter Weekend Retreat if you haven't first attended one as a participant. You can find a list of upcoming Encounters and Training Sessions at the Master's Plan web site.

3. **Pray through** on it until you know the Lord has definitely called you to do this in your church. It's not for everybody. Not every pastor or church is willing to *pray* the price or *pay* the price for such a powerful transition. This is a dynamic model that is all-consuming in so many ways.

You need to know that you know that you know that God has told you that you *must* do this. Wait until that clear call comes from God. Never get into this model unless the Holy Spirit makes it abundantly obvious that you can do nothing else.

4. **Ask a Nazarene pastor** who is into this vision to coach you. There is a lot to think about. Save yourself a ton of time and tears by having a pastor who is a bit ahead of you coach you in this model. More than with any other model we are aware of, you truly do need a personal coach. You will have a lot of questions along the way. A Master's Plan coach can really help you out. Pray weekly with your coach about what you are attempting to do for God. Follow his or her counsel. The two of you will put ten thousand to flight![1]

5. **If you are married, wait until your spouse is on board.** If this is God's plan for you, then God is calling your spouse into it as well. Maybe this is God's plan for you but the timing is not right. Wait until your spouse is also excited about it. Pray until this happens. Some pastors who are successfully implementing this model waited up to two years until God moved the hearts of their spouses. This is a crucial step.

6. **Prayerfully introduce it to your board.** Take your time. Do it right. This vision is so profound and so pervasive that you will want a proper *buy-in* by the leadership of your church. At Anaheim First Church, we spent over six months introducing our board leadership to the vision. We used books, literature, and personal sharing. We even attended a conference together with over half of the board. Afterward, there were meals with each board member and their spouses to share the vision, engage in joint prayer, and carry out much discussion.

7. **Avoid the use of the phrase "G12"** in your public discussions. Call it "The Master's Plan" or "The Discipleship Model" or some other generic name. For some reason, some people get worked up over the phrase G12. There are many negative things people can run into on the Internet when they Google "G12."

8. **Avoid the five worst mistakes** that pastors make in implementing the Master's Plan.

- Don't go back to your church and announce from the pulpit, "We are going to be a Master's Plan church, and you are all going to be leading groups of twelve—for the rest of your life!" This is fun but dumb! Some pastors have really regretted taking this course.

- Don't run out and just grab twelve guys to be your disciples. Jesus wasn't in a rush to get his twelve, and neither should you. Many pastors take four to five years or longer to complete their twelve. Pastor Adalberto Herrera of Cali, Colombia, had not completed his twelve even after being in this model for seven years. If you go out and merely get twelve guys, you'll end up regretting picking some of them. You'll probably be eighteen months or more into this vision before you begin to pick your twelve. Truly wait on God. There is no rush.

- Don't try to implement this plan too fast. Take your time. Pray. Pray each step through. This is one area in church life you pray you won't be blown away with speedy, runaway success. The sheer stress of success can kill you if it comes too quickly or too soon. Build your credibility with your people. If you have to, choose a few key leaders and work underground for a while before you ever go public.

- Don't dismantle other ministries such as Sunday School, existing small groups, or Sunday night services. Find ways to work within these systems or at least work around them for a while. Let the Master's Plan be something that comes up from underneath like a mighty groundswell. Existing ministries will either move over to the Master's Plan or wither in time, dying of their own natural causes. At our church, we expect to have some traditional Sunday School classes for the few who want and need that format until Jesus comes. Schedule the Master's Plan courses at times when other ministries don't conflict. Offer them as a Wednesday night, Sunday night, or Sunday School option. Anytime people are already used to coming to church is a good time choice.

- Don't try to do it by yourself. Work with others who are implementing this model. You will learn so much from each other. You save yourself massive amounts of effort and hassle by working with others who are tracking the same vision. Form a task force with key leaders who are beginning to catch the vision. Work with and listen to these leaders.

9. **Preach disciple-making principles and concepts.** You can, in time, change the whole culture and tone of your church by your faithful prayers and preaching. Create a *thirst* in your people for training in becoming disciple-makers. From the pulpit, tell them it how it is God's will and his destiny for them to be involved in the Great Commission, because it is.

10. **Meet with your key leaders weekly,** casting your vision before them. Pray for favor in their eyes for the vision of the Master's Plan.

11. **Have your leadership go to a conference or an Encounter with you** *after you* have already been to an Encounter. Let them be around other laypeople who are excited about this vision.

12. **Prepare a strong prayer foundation in your church** before you attempt to implement the Master's Plan. Failure to do this will equal failure. You will not succeed without this basic component in place. It is foundational and absolutely essential. *Don't leave home without it!*

13. **Prepare yourself and your leadership for unprecedented spiritual warfare.** Satan and his minions hate any model of disciple-making that engages God's people in multiplication. Be warned—you are in for the fight of your life. Many spiritual casualties have occurred as pastors have tried to implement this earth-changing model in their churches. Pastor after pastor has shared with us how they faced spiritual warfare like they had never known before once they committed to implementing the Master's Plan. Satan is faithful to fight this like nothing else, but our Heavenly Father is even more faithful. He will help you if he has truly led you into this powerful, multiplying vision.

14. **Let your leadership read this book.** Discuss it together, pray about it together, then do it together. If possible, take a few key leaders to Cali, Colombia. They will never be the same.

15. **Keep broken and humble before the Lord.** Spend more time on your knees that you are used to spending. Many Master's Plan pastors spend three hours or more a day

in prayer. No other model we are familiar with demands so much—

- Personal purity and holiness.
- Holy Spirit anointing.
- Fervent prayer and intercession.
- Divine protection and favor.
- Spiritual warfare.
- Brokenness and humility before God.
- Teachability and openness to correction.
- Personal modeling.
- Time! This is a very time-intensive methodology, but it is well worth it!

Remember—please *pray through* on this before you attempt to implement this powerful multiplying plan. Wait until you know God's will on this vital matter. You definitely don't want to adopt this model until God calls you into it!

ten

What God Is Doing in the Church of the Nazarene Through the Master's Plan in North America

✦ Our Lord is beginning to do some amazing things in the Church of the Nazarene through this dynamic model. In addition to what's going on in the great church in Cali, Colombia, Nazarene pastors and leaders are beginning to implement the principles articulated in this powerful vision. This chapter highlights just a few of the churches that are truly being transformed by God's vision of the multiplication of disciple-makers.

Here, in ministers' own words, are some stories that are just beginning to be written.

Cerritos, California—Pastor Rollie Miller of Crossroads Multicultural Church of the Nazarene:

When we began to use the Master's Plan in Cerritos, it made an immediate impact on the congregation. The Master's Plan looks different in an established church than it does in a new start or a restart, either of which can be dedicated to this direction from the beginning of their ministry. When we started the Master's Plan, Cerritos was a well-established church of two hundred, with all the programs and emphases of an established Nazarene congregation.

I decided that we would start it "underneath" the existing programs rather than replace them with something else that would be perceived as programming. I packaged and sold it as leadership training for the first two years. We started the first year with board members, cell group leaders, and staff—about forty people in the first group. The second year we invited new board members and others in leadership roles in the church—about thirty-five more of our best people. Because we started this with our leaders in those first two years, the Master's Plan took root in the culture of our church and quickly became not only accepted but expected for those who were going to lead in the church. Using this strategy has several advantages:

1. *It gives the leadership of the church an understanding of what the Master's Plan is all about.* There is no ambiguity or uncertainty about it when it is mentioned, because virtually every leader in the congregation has been through it.

2. *It creates ownership and investment in the Master's Plan by the leadership of the church.* When you start with the leadership, they are immediate insiders. They have experienced this, not just learned about it, and they are sold on its value.

3. *It builds camaraderie in your leaders.* Military and top-quality sports programs capitalize on shared suffering to bond their participants. The discipline and sacrifice of traveling together through the Master's Plan gives your leadership a common foundational experience and quickly develops a shared culture that becomes the basis for unity and trust.

4. *It develops critical mass.* By the end of the second year, seventy-five of our best people, in a church of two hundred, had come through the Master's Plan.

This was no longer just something for the elite of the congregation. More than half of our adult population had come through the training. An enthusiastic missionary force was now in place in our congregation who urged others to be a part of this.

5. *It creates a spirit of expectancy.* When lives are visibly changed by something like an Encounter Retreat and the people in the congregation see that change and hear about it, they began to get excited about the possibilities in their own lives.

The Cerritos Church has grown from two hundred to over five hundred in Sunday morning worship services in its three years of implementing the Master's Plan.

Ceres, California—Pastor Joe Holloway of Valley View Church of the Nazarene:

In 2008, when I interviewed at Valley View Church, I submitted my outline of the Master's Plan as my vision for ministry. In our discussions we considered the challenges of placing discipleship as central to our ministry. In everything we discussed, it was a powerful presence that settled upon the room as the vision of Matthew 28:19-20 started becoming a possible reality in the minds of those present.

My wife, Ogla, and I left that meeting knowing God had set the appointment as their hearts were beating as one with ours—making ministry deeply relational. Though the circumstances were riddled with challenges, we all felt God's leading to become disciple-makers of disciple-makers together.

When I arrived, we were averaging around sixty to seventy people in worship. Our most recent report, for September 2010, was 154 in worship—and we have yet to fully employ the Master's Plan. Our cell groups, which we call life groups, begin in March 2011.

I have added a personal component to the Master's Plan that embraces a preparatory path of one-to-one mentoring. We use materials that establish the basics of our faith in Christ Jesus and start the journey of closer relationships. We start looking for those who are ready to meet their divine appointment with God—the Encounter. I feel this has become an essential part as it warms people up to relational accountability.

Our first Encounter took place eleven months after our arriving. During the first year, we trained leadership in the concepts of relational discipleship and the Master's Plan. In October 2009 we led twenty leaders through their first Encounter. Seventeen continued on in the follow-up training we call The Master's Plan School. As a result, we now have forty-nine people in one-to-one mentoring, all being mentored by those who first went through the Encounter.

In our second Encounter, January 2010, we had twenty-nine attending. From that second Encounter, eleven have continued in The Master's Plan School. Our third Encounter as of this writing is only one week away, with nineteen attending and several returning from the second Encounter to restart their journey to become disciple-makers. This Encounter will be led mostly by those who attended the first Encounter. I believe this must get out of my hands in order for the Master's Plan to truly have the impact God intends.

Our Master's Plan School will be led by that first group as well. By our next Encounter in April of 2011, I fully expect to only lead two sessions. What a blessing to see ministry in the hands of passionate lay disciple-makers!

At present I have five men who meet weekly with me for discipleship. My wife, Ogla, has nine women she meets with weekly. They are all in prayer and preparation to move from being mentors to disciple-makers. We expect our people to seek God for three people they will commit to disciple. We are seeing this become a reality.

How do you explain the impact and energy that continue due to the process of the Master's Plan? Truly you cannot. It must be experienced. I have labeled this experience the twenty-first-century revival. Accountable relationships that begin amid the power of the healing, liberating touch of God are bound together deeply. They are passionate for others to experience it. I have watched with tear-clouded eyes on the Sunday following the Encounter as those who attended testify. From teenagers to octogenarians, I have heard their telling of the change, healing, and renewal they experience.

I will paraphrase one of those "saints" whose brother-in-law started our church in the 1950s: "I was just going through the motions of my faith. I have always been faithful and have learned the truth, but since the Encounter and The Master's Plan School, I have become alive in my walk with the Lord."

One teen spoke of how he now understands his father and his father's faith. He used words like "respect," "love," and "gratitude" to tell all of us how his father had led him. The congregation had watched the rebellious teen disrespect that very same father. Oh, God still continues to transform that young man! Too many stories—too little space. This I know: God continues having divine appointments with his people each week.

What makes me so invested in the Master's Plan? Teenagers, young parents, the middle-aged, and those who thought they were winding down their ministry all become focused and united on one goal: disciple-making! This is fulfilling the will of the Father. For this I am deeply humbled and appreciative. Never has ministry been so fulfilling as it is now. May the Lord be praised for such a powerful and clear calling as this!

Galesburg, Illinois—Pastor Ron Scarlett of Galesburg First Church of the Nazarene:

The Master's Plan for Galesburg First has been the discipleship answer we had been looking for. It begins with an Encounter and then takes those who attend the Encounter through forty weeks of discipleship training. The Encounter in and of itself has been a mini-revival, only with greater results. It is life-changing. It compels us to look at ourselves spiritually and takes us from salvation to sanctification. It has transformed whole families.

A mother who had not been coming to church for very long attended with her husband and brought her unchurched daughter with her. Their lives were so radically changed that her other daughter saw the difference in their lives. She said, "I wanted what they have." She started coming to church, attended our next Encounter, and her life was changed as well. Her son saw the difference in his mother and sisters, so he started coming to church with his family. They have accepted Christ and are attending our next Encounter. The entire family has been baptized and has started its own small-group Bible study, which one of the daughters leads.

Those who have been in the church for years have testified to being set free from things in their past that they thought they would never be free from. They are thrilled to see how so many lives are being changed, and for the first time they understand what the power of the Holy Spirit can do in their own lives. The Master's Plan is the first discipleship study that starts with getting people spiritually ready and then leads each person through Bible study to become what Jesus has commanded us all to become—a disciple.

Pekin, Illinois—Pastors Lloyd and Kim Brock of First Church of the Nazarene:

Pekin First Church of the Nazarene is a congregation of about five hundred with an eighty-year heritage in the Church of the Nazarene. The church is alive and growing and is very community-oriented. The Master's Plan is the answer to the need of new believers becoming deep, strong, committed followers of Christ. Also it is helping long-time believers to see the need to *intentionally* pour their lives into those of other believers.

We have seen the powerful impact of Encounters as they have ignited new life in long-time believers and new

Christians. Sanctification has been the clear result of every Encounter. About twenty percent of our congregation have gone through an Encounter. Currently we have forty-nine individuals who are in the discipling courses. We are excited about how God is using the Master's Plan in an established church as a way to fruitfully live out the Great Commission.

My church, Anaheim First, is over eighty-five years old. The church had been in a twenty-two-year decline when we began the Master's Plan. Today prayer is becoming the priority of the leadership of our church. The church is starting to slowly turn around. We have one hundred eighty-five languages spoken within a ten-minute drive of our church! The challenge is huge. But the Master's Plan is giving us hope and a model to follow. We are praying that someday God will give us twelve ethnic congregations all moving in the Master's Plan model and vision.

Today God has given us a dynamic Spanish ministry that is reaching the neighborhoods around our church where the zip codes are made up of eighty-seven percent Spanish-speaking people. Our Spanish family is actively planting two daughter churches using the Master's Plan. These churches are being "led" by laymen who are being discipled by the men I disciple.

We have seen over fifty people sanctified at our Encounters. Over fifty have been taught and trained to be disciple-makers. I am discipling six men in my lead group, and my wife, Connie, is discipling eight ladies in her lead group. God is about to do something great in our midst.

We have held a number of Pastors' Training days in the Master's Plan and have hosted Encounters in both Spanish and English. We have successfully conducted a Youth Encounter. We have seen phenomenal healings, deliverances, and glorious sanctifications through the Master's Plan!

Appendix

Key Qualities and Characteristics to Look for or Consider as You Begin to Select Your Disciples Who Will Make Disciples

Whom should you select for the members of your twelve?

In 2 Timothy 2:2, Paul tells Timothy to find "faithful men" who can teach others. Working off the acrostic "F.A.I.T.H.F.U.L. M.E.N.," we have a suggested starting list of qualities that would be important to look for in potential disciple-makers.

F = faithful. This refers to people who are faithful to Jesus and faithful to his Word. They are faithful in service. They "out-serve" everybody. They are fully consecrated to God. They are surrendered to Jesus with a truly sanctified heart. They are faithful in the sense that they are "full of faith." They are constant, consistent people of their word, full of integrity and pure. You can trust them. They follow through on what they say they will do. They are committed and sold out to Jesus. They have proven to be sacrificial to the cause of Christ. They are faithful to you as their leader. They have been faithful to the discipleship vision and model that God has given you to implement. They have attended the courses, classes, and retreats. They have been faithful in the homework and assignments. They have been faithful to memorize Scripture. They have been faithful in little things and they are about to be entrusted with much[1]—the discipling of a young Christian.

A = available. They really want to meet with you, and they are willing to rearrange their schedules to make top-quality time happen with you. You don't have to chase them down to meet with them. They are very good about returning phone calls to you and have proven that meeting with you regularly is a very high priority to them. They know that ongoing discipling can't happen without regular, unrushed appointments with you. They make themselves available to you.

I = intimate with Jesus. They are constantly drawing closer and closer to Jesus. They passionately love him and sacrifice for him. They are people of prayer and worship. They love being with Jesus. Obeying him is their highest priority. Their greatest passion is to be like Jesus and to please him at all costs.

T = teachable. They are teachable. They are "correctable." They allow you to speak into their hearts. They allow you to correct them and even invite you to do it. They see the value of listening to you and learning what God is teaching you. They change when you ask them to change something that is detrimental to their witnessing or their walk with God. They want to be "coached." They don't know it all. They have a basic humility that causes them to listen well and apply what they are learning. They respond well to correction, reproof, and rebuke. They invite your constructive criticism.

They are hungry to change if necessary to be more like Jesus or to be more effective at disciple-making.

H = heart and passion for the vision. They really get it. They are sold out to the cause of Christ and the mission of making disciples who make disciples. They see the value of the Master's Plan and are excited about implementing it. They "see" beyond what is going on—and they are excited about what God is getting ready to do. They talk about the vision of making disciples of Jesus. They are willing to re-arrange their lives and values to pursue the high calling of making disciples.

F = fruitful. They win souls. They have a passion for lost people that results in fervent intercession and supplication for those without Christ. They are people of influence. They make things happen. Their life groups actually grow and at-tract people. They are successful at soulwinning and con-necting new Christians into their group and into the church. They are willing to be pruned by the Father for the sake of producing more fruit. They are not content with the status quo and want to continually be improving and abiding in Christ so that they can win more souls. They truly believe that Jesus meant it when he said that his Father was glori-fied when we bear *much fruit.*[2] They are willing to try new strategies to "by all means save some" (1 Cor. 9:22). They are willing to set goals and pray and work to see these goals met. They are willing to be trained to be more effective at reach-ing people for Jesus. They believe that Jesus can make them "100x" people who are truly fruitful for our Lord. They are not happy or content with their present level of fruitfulness.

U = under authority. They see the value of being under authority and recognize that effectiveness, power, authority, leadership, blessing, protection, and much fruitfulness result from properly being under godly authority. They joyfully submit to you just as to the Lord. They see the value of submission. They realize that they can't be good leaders if they haven't proven to be good followers. They know that only those under authority will be given godly authority. They covet proper covering and the protection that comes from being under the authority that God has given them to honor and follow.

L = love. They love you, and you love them. They have a love for Jesus and a love for people. There is a natural affinity, affection, and attraction (for close friendship) between you and them. You really enjoy being with them and hanging out with them. They want to be close to you. They want to be in your twelve. They are willing to pay almost any cost and do almost anything to help you accomplish God's vision for reaching the lost world.

M = mighty in spirit. They are mighty in prayer and intercession. They are mighty in spiritual warfare. The power of their godly spirit can influence and motivate others. They are mighty in God. Their spirit is moved and powered by God. These are "God's generals"!

E = emulatable. They live a life worth emulating. They have solid integrity. They have a strong, pure, righteous spirit. You know you can trust new Christians with them. They can properly say, along with Paul, "Imitate me as I imitate Christ."[3] They are good role models as well as Christians, spouses, parents, and servant leaders. They have irreproachable character.

N = named and nominated by God. As you fervently prayed over them, God chose them for you. Jesus spent all night in prayer seeking his Father's direction regarding the selection of his original twelve.[4] God will guide you, and of all the qualities mentioned, this is probably the "trump card" that is more important than the others. If God has called you to work with someone and include him or her in your inner circle of disciples, then you need to obey God, even if he or she is missing some of the other qualities and characteristics. God will hand-pick your disciples for you—if you let him. Begin now to ask God to give you your disciples.

For our ladies—you can use the acrostic "F.A.I.T.H.F.U.L. W.O.M.E.N.," adding the following "W" and "O":

W = winsome, attractive personality. They are gentle, loving, compassionate, Christlike, and full of mercy and grace. They are "likeable"—other ladies just like being around them. They are good friends. They are full of encouragement and favor for others.

O = obedient to Jesus. They pray and they obey. They are serious about obeying their Lord Jesus no matter what it costs.

No doubt this seems like an impossible and idealistic list. I almost feel like saying, "Man, if I can find people who are all of this, I shouldn't be discipling *them*—they should be discipling *me*!" or "If they have all of these qualities *before* we begin working with them, do they even need us to disciple them at all?"

The truth is that probably very few people before they are discipled will exhibit all these qualities or characteristics. Peter and John didn't necessarily have all of them before Jesus called them to follow him. But our Lord must have seen the potential in them, and, of course, the Father told him who to pick for his twelve. They weren't perfect before or after Jesus spent three years with them. But they all had incredible potential that the Holy Spirit could use and develop. Jesus looked for the right heart-attitudes in his disciples.

Your disciple doesn't have to be totally perfect and totally Christlike before you begin discipling him or her. However, with the discernment of the Holy Spirit, we can trust that the Lord can show us the heart and potential in each of the people we will serve and lead. These qualities or characteristics may be only in "embryonic form" when you first begin pouring your life into your special disciple. God will help you to help him or her develop in these areas.

Hopefully you can see many or most of these qualities in the potential disciple whom you are prayerfully considering. God can help you to train and coach your God-chosen disciple in the areas where maybe he or she needs to grow and develop some more.

On the other hand, if you can't imagine the potential disciple *ever* measuring up in any of these areas—you probably shouldn't enter into a discipling relationship at this level with the person. You can still love and bless him or her and at points coach him or her, but you would probably be wise not to invest too much of your limited time with someone who doesn't exhibit any of these qualities or exhibits only a very few of them.

God will guide you as you fervently seek his will and direction in this matter. God has already chosen whom he wants you to disciple. He already knows the person's name. Ask him to lead you to the people he has chosen for you to invest your life into—for a long time. No wonder Jesus spent all night in prayer before he chose his twelve!

One more thought: this is a good checklist for each of us. If this is what we should be looking for in someone else, we ought to ask Jesus to make us examples in each of these key areas so that we can model them for the disciples Jesus gives us.

Look over the list and check the ones that you feel good or strong in—and note the ones that you need to work on with God's help. By God's grace and power, we can all be *faithful men or women.*

A Comparison of Addition vs. Multiplication

Let's imagine two scenarios.

Scenario One: Addition

Imagine if by your phenomenal evangelism gifts you became a Super Evangelist and could personally add one million people to the kingdom of God every year! Wow! That would be awesome! Even more fantastic (and more unrealistic), imagine if none of them fell away—your retention rate was one hundred percent. It would look like this:

	Led to Christ	Grand Total
Year 1	1,000,000	1,000,000 believers
Year 2	1,000,000	2,000,000
Year 3	1,000,000	3,000,000
Year 24	1,000,000	24,000,000

You would be *adding* one million a year to the church of Jesus. Praise God—that would be fantastic! Think of it: twenty-four million believers in twenty-four years!

Scenario Two: Multiplication by the Principle of Twelve

Imagine if by God's help you could raise up twelve disciples in three years. (This is how long it took Jesus to raise up his twelve) Then, as you continue to pour your life into those twelve and disciple them in the following three-year cycle, God would help them to each raise up his or her twelve disciples. If this chain of disciple-making would continue unbroken, in three years you would have twelve, in six years you would have one hundred forty-four, and so on. It would look something like this:

Years 1-3	12
Years 4-6	144
Years 7-9	1,728
Years 10-12	20,736
Years 13-15	248,832
Years 16-18	2,985,984
Years 19-21	35,831,808
Years 22-24	429,981,696
Grand total	**469,070,940**

—and after that it *really* gets exciting!

Contrasting Scenario One with Scenario Two

By year twenty-four, the Super Evangelist, by adding one million each year, would have reached a grand total of *twenty-four million people.* In that same time, the disciple-maker would have reached and discipled only twelve—but as the chain of multiplication had continued, by year twenty-four there would be *469,070,940 disciple-making disciple-makers!*

At this rate it would take the Super Evangelist over *445 more years* (if that were possible!) to catch up to what the disciple-maker and his or her twelve and their twelves had accomplished in twenty-four years.

Jesus had a more efficient and effective plan than mere addition. His Master's Plan involved multiplication! Raise up twelve and release them to do the same—make disciples who will make disciples. Multiplication has always been in the heart and mind of the Father.

Note: Even if it took you *five years* to get your twelve disciples and five years after that to get the one hundred forty-four, and so on, it would still be phenomenal. It would look like this:

Years 1-5	12
Years 6-10	144
Years 11-15	1,728
Years 16-20	20,736
Years 21-25	248,832
Years 26-30	2,985,984
Years 31-35	35,831,808
Years 36-40	429,981,696
Total	**469,070,940**

Not bad for a forty-year ministry!

Faith Scenario

Take the chart above and imagine if one Nazarene pastor would set the *reasonable goal* of doing just what Jesus did—*taking three years to make twelve disciples* who would be trained in turn to make twelve more disciples each in the following three years and so on, and the chain were to continue.

The first person who started this chain would still just be pouring his or her life into his or her twelve faithful people! This is a reasonable, attainable goal. There are pastors walking around on this planet who already are working and praying for their 20,736—and God has given this many disciples of disciples to them! By God's power and his supernatural help—why can't I do this?

Philippians 4:13—"I can do all things through Christ who strengthens me" (NKJV).

What if *two* people did this, or a hundred? I got pretty excited about the possibilities of this really happening. This seems like a goal worthy of our great King Jesus!

Thank God for all addition growth, but imagine what multiplication growth could mean for the kingdom of God! Our God is a God of multiplication, and he wants to multiply Christlike disciples through you and me!

If the whole concept of discipling twelve who in turn disciple twelve more, and so on, is too overwhelming for you to imagine, think about multiplication on its most basic scale, that is, "each one reach one."

If everybody in your church would reach just one person for Jesus in the course of a year—your church would double every year! And some would be enabled by God through their gifts and graces to reach more than one a year!

If we added a time dimension to the "each one reach one" concept, then imagine what could happen in a few years. Let's think about this most basic scenario: What if one faithful, Christlike Christian began to pray and ask God to help him or her to reach at least one person for Christ this year.

Then, when that new convert is won to Christ, that new Christian is taught and discipled faithfully by the one who led him or her to Christ—who teaches (disciples) and helps him or her in one year's time so that at the end of that year, that new disciple of Jesus could also reach one and teach him or her to become a Christlike disciple of Jesus. This slow, methodical, multiplication model could take the entire world for Christ in a single lifetime!

Each one reach one and teach one—in one year! The multiplication is slow at first. But try to wrap your brain around what could possibly happen if the discipleship chain is unbroken and the multiplication happens each year.

The reality of exponential multiplication is unbelievably powerful. It all starts relatively slowly, but eventually it explodes with earth-shaking results.

Imagine what would happen if the following progression of *each one reach one and teach one each year* would become a reality. Think of it this way: What would happen if just one Christian took the call of Christ to disciple-making seriously and won one person to Christ in a year's time and spent that year training and teaching him or her to do the same with one more person? At the end of one year there would be two disciple-makers (1 + 1 = 2).

Then, if the process were repeated the following year— the two faithful disciple-makers would each win one more and disciple those new believers to the point at which in a year's time they could continue the process—now we would have four disciple-makers (2 + 2 = 4). If this continued, look at what would happen.

The Exponential Multiplication Chart

Year		Disciples
1	1+1 =	2
2		4
3		8
4		16
5		32
6		64
7		128
8		256
9		512
10		1,024
11		2,048
12		4,096
13		8,192
14		16,384
15		32,768
16		65,536
17		131,072
18		262,144
19		524,288
20		1,048,576—not bad for a twenty-year ministry! Over one million disciples for Jesus!
21		2,097,152
22		4,194,304
23		8,358,608
24		16,777,216
25		33,554,432
26		67,108,864
27		134,217,928
28		268,435,856
29		536,871,712
30		1,073,743,424—one billion discipled disciple-makers of Jesus in thirty years!
31		2,147,486,848
32		4,294,973,696
33		8,589,947,392 (At this writing there are six and a half billion people on planet earth.)

The whole world could be reached for Jesus in a single lifetime of ministry if just *one* person would get serious about disciple-making with one more person—and the chain of multiplication would continue!

In fact, there are hundreds of millions of born-again, Spirit-filled believers in Jesus in the world today. Looking at the chart, you could easily go to year twenty-eight —268,435,856—and see that if each one of them would reach one more and the chain continued for five years or so, the entire world could be reached for Jesus! (It is estimated that there are easily over 600,000,000 born-again believers in Jesus on planet earth right now.)

Today over fifty-one percent of the continent of Africa are born-again believers in Jesus. Simple logic tells us that if each one of them would just reach one more, the entire continent could belong to Jesus in a few months. Multiplication is powerful!

Our God of multiplication knows this. When will we figure it out? Jesus knew this all along. That is why he diligently poured his life into a few who would in turn pour their lives into a few more who would do the same—and the world would be won! This is the Master's Plan.

Twelve Common Errors Encountered in the Master's Plan
by Pastor Diego Feraro

Pastor Diego Feraro was a part of the Cali Church of the Nazarene's growth from day one. He became a part of Pastor Adalberto Herrera's lead group of twelve. God called Diego to come as a missionary to California and plant a church on the Southern California District under the leadership of District Superintendent John Denney. He is an accomplished implementer of the Master's Plan model of disciple-making.

He is well aware of the most common errors that pastors and leaders encounter when they try to implement the Master's Plan. Here are his conclusions:

Truth 1: The passion must be in the heart of the senior pastor.
The error: Believing that the passion comes from the fad of the day—or the program of the day.

Truth 2: One must keep the integrity of the Master's Plan.
The error: Believing that any idea or adaptation is okay.

Truth 3: The entire church—all ministries—must share the same vision.
The error: Each ministry can do as they please.

Truth 4: We must dedicate full-time attention to the development and implementation of the vision of the Master's Plan.
The error: Not dedicating full time to the implementation and the development of the vision.

Truth 5: Cells are primary.
The error: The belief that cells are secondary.

Truth 6: We must make the visitors feel wanted, loved, needed, and at home.
The error: Allowing visitors to make it on their own and find their own way.

Truth 7: The Encounter Weekend Retreat is only a single step in the Master's Plan.
The error: The belief that the Encounter is "everything" to the Master's Plan and can stand alone.

Truth 8: It is important to invite only the key leaders to the first Encounter Weekend Retreat.

The error: Inviting the whole church to the first Encounter.

Truth 9: We need a dedicated team of intercessors to pray for the vision.

The error: Not having a dedicated team of intercessors to pray for the vision.

Truth 10: There is a need to pastor and care for all the people in the church, even those not in the Master's Plan.

The error: Neglecting the people in the church who are not in the Master's Plan.

Truth 11: Growth will come only after the vision of the Master's Plan has taken root and is functioning in the lives of the people.

The error: The belief that the growth of the church will come immediately with the implementation of the vision of the Master's Plan.

Truth 12: We must meet each week in the closed-cell lead group (original leaders and disciples of the pastor) to continue to motivate and cast vision.

The error: Not meeting weekly with the original cell leaders (closed cell) for motivation and vision.

Do-Whatever-It-Takes Prayer

Lord,

- *Do whatever it takes* to break me, keep me broken before you, keep me humble and on my knees in desperate prayer, praying without ceasing, in total dependency upon you. Break me so you can bless me and make me a blessing (Gen. 32:24-32).

- *Do whatever it takes* to prune me and my ministry to produce more fruit for your glory (John 15:2, 8).

- *Do whatever it takes* to make me a better listener and to hear your voice better and obey you more completely and follow you today (John 10:27).

- *Do whatever it takes* to make me like Jesus—who was perfected through his sufferings and who learned obedience through his sufferings (Heb. 2:10; 5:8).

- *Do whatever it takes* to make me as holy and as pure as you can make somebody this side of heaven (Heb. 12:14; Matt. 5:8).

- *Do whatever it takes* to keep me from sinning today (1 John 2:1; 3:6-10).

- *Do whatever it takes* to make me a true disciple of you, Jesus, and to make me an effective disciple-maker of disciple-makers (Matt. 28:19-20).

- *Do whatever it takes* to help me set you continually before me today and to keep my mind stayed on you (Ps. 16:8; Isa. 26:3).

- *Do whatever it takes* to make me as fruitful as you have appointed me to be (John 15:1-16).

- *Do whatever it takes* to make me a wise and effective soul winner (Prov. 11:30).

- *Do whatever it takes* to make me a righteous follower who can pray powerful, fervent, effectual prayers that avail much. Jesus, make me an intercessor like you! (James 5:16).

- *Do whatever it takes* to make me abide in you, your love, and in your Word (John 15:1-16).

- *Do whatever it takes* to train me to live as you lived, precious Jesus—you never spoke one word or did anything on your own initiative, but you spoke only what the Father told you to speak, did only what the Father told you to do and what you saw the Father doing (John 5:19-30; 8:26-29, 40, 42; 12:49-50).

- *Do whatever it takes,* dear Jesus, to break me and help me to enter into the fellowship of your sufferings. Pour a little of your pain into my heart so that I can weep as you weep. Help me to feel what you feel and weep with you, sharing your tears and feeling the hurt that is in your heart for broken and lost people. Cry your tears through my eyes. Break me so that I can weep with hurting people who are weeping and enter into the fellowship of their suffering (Phil. 3:10; Rom. 12:15).

- *Do whatever it takes,* Lord, to make me willing to be your living sacrifice, your burnt offering, or your drink offering to be poured out before you. By your grace make me willing to be offered up before you until with joy I can say, "I am ready to be offered up for you, Lord Jesus!"

- *Do whatever it takes,* Lord Jesus, for if you do not do it, I surely cannot do any of these things on my own! (John 15:4-5).

Lord, I beg you—*do whatever it takes!*

Jesus, I believe that as you break me I will be phenomenally blessed and become a blessing to others. I know that *brokenness = blessing.* I know that I cannot take people into your deepest truths unless you, Lord, have broken me. Break me, in your tenderness and because you love me so much, so that I can go deeply with you. I know that there is no other way to get into the depths of God but through brokenness! So in love, break me further, I pray.

Let me be "broken and spilled out" for you, sweet Jesus, and for others who are broken, lost, hurting, and dying.

Lord, please let me keep myself as brokenhearted for lost souls as you are, and let your fragrance spread around through my brokenness as a crushed rose gives off its fragrance.

Now speak to my waiting, open, willing, obedient, purified, broken, desperate heart. Awaken my ears to hear your voice. Open my ears to hear your heart. Give me the ears and tongue of a disciple (Isa. 50:4-5).

Do whatever it takes, Lord!

Jesus, I am yours, and I belong to you. I am yours, O God. I am yours. Do whatever it takes in me, Lord Jesus, and help me to bear it with joy, hope, faith, love, wisdom, and grace—and without self-pity. Help me to believe that great joy, great blessing, and great fruitfulness will result because of this prayer that I pray with all my heart.

And, Lord, with all of this breaking you will allow into my life—please remember that we need some *breakthroughs*. Your name is "Baal Perazim," "The Lord of the breakthroughs" (2 Sam. 5:20; 1 Chron. 14:11). I desperately need you to break through for me and for us today! Please, dear God—give us a breakthrough today in some area that will encourage us and help us to carry on, trusting you for more breakthroughs and deliverances and victories. In the breakings give us some breakthroughs—today, I pray, please, Lord Jesus! Through it all, Lord Jesus, help me to delight in you and to be so conscious of your presence. I pray all of this *in the mighty, mighty name of Jesus Christ of Nazareth.* Amen and Amen.

John Wesley's Covenant Prayer[5]

I am no longer my own, but Yours.
Put me to what You will,
Rank me with whom You will.
Put me to doing,
Put me to suffering.
Let me be employed for You or laid aside for You,
Exalted by You or brought low by You.
Let me have all things,
Let me have nothing.
I freely and heartily yield all things to Your pleasure and
    disposal.
And now, O glorious and blessed God,
Father, Son, and Holy Spirit,
You are mine, and I am Yours.
So be it.
And the covenant which I have made on earth,
Let it be ratified in heaven.
Amen.

Notes

Chapter 1

1. Proverbs 29:18: "Where there is no vision, the people perish: but he that keepeth the law, happy is he" (KJV).

2. J. Edwin Hartill, *Principles of Biblical Hermeneutics* (Grand Rapids: Zondervan Publishing House, 1947), 70. Dr. A. T. Pierson is quoted here saying this about the Law of First Mention: "This is a law we have long since noted, and have never yet found it to fail. The first occurrence of a word, expression, or utterance is the key to its subsequent meaning, or it will be a guide to ascertaining the essential truth connected with it."

3. Ibid., 70.

4. Galatians 3:6-14; Romans 2:28-29; 4:16.

5. Mark 4:8: "Other seeds fell into the good soil, and as they grew up and increased, they yielded a crop and produced thirty, sixty, and a hundredfold."

6. John 15:2, 4, 5, 8, 16.

7. Larry Stockstill, *Every Member a Multitude!* (Baton Rouge, La.: International Cell Conference, September 14, 2004), 13.

8. Genesis 6:1-12.

9. Stockstill, *Every Member a Multitude!* 13.

Chapter 2

1. Personal interviews with Pastors Adalberto and Nineye Herrera between 2005 and 2010 and Pastor Jaime Restrepo in 2010. Also material was quoted from the Cali Church of the Nazarene's web site.

Chapter 3

1. General Superintendent Jerry Porter speaking at the Discipleship Summit in Destin, Florida, May 2010.

2. Cesar Castellanos, *Successful Leadership Through the Government of 12* (San Jose, Calif.: Spirit-Filled Productions, 2002), 12.

3. Colin Dye, "Fulfilling the Mandate," *G12 Harvest Magazine*, Europe Edition, Special Edition, 2001, 5.

4. Ibid.

5. Castellanos, *Successful Leadership*, 43.

6. Ibid.

7. Personal interview with Larry Stockstill in the Atlanta airport on November 8, 2006.

8. Larry Stockstill, *Every Member a Multitude!*

Chapter 5

1. Mark 9:35: "After Jesus sat down and told the twelve disciples to gather around him, he said, 'If you want the place of honor, you must become a slave and serve others!'" (CEV).

2. Acts 19:1-10.

Chapter 6

1. Luke 6:12-13: "It was at this time that He went off to the mountain to pray, and He spent the whole night in prayer to God. And when day came, He called His disciples to Him and chose twelve of them, whom He also named as apostles."

2. Corinthians 11:1: "Be imitators of me, just as I also am of Christ."

3. Allen Hadidian, *Successful Discipling* (Chicago: Moody Press, 1979), 29-30.

4. John Wesley, "List of Poetical Works," in *The Works of John Wesley*, ed. Thomas Jackson, vol. 14 (Kansas City: Beacon Hill Press of Kansas City, 1986), 321. Originally published in *The Works of John Wesley* (London: Wesleyan Methodist Book Room, 1872).

Chapter 7

1. John 13:34; Romans 12:10, 16; 13:8; 14:13; 15:7, 14; 16:16; 1 Corinthians 1:10; 16:20; 2 Corinthians 13:12; Galatians 5:13; Ephesians 4:2, 32; 5:19, 21; Colossians 3:13, 16; 1 Thessalonians 4:9, 18; 5:11; Hebrews 3:13; 10:24, 25; James 4:11; 5:9; 1 Peter 1:22; 4:9; 5:5, 14; 1 John 1:7; 3:11, 23; 4:7, 11, 12; 2 John 1:5.

Chapter 9

1. Deuteronomy 32:30: "How could one chase a thousand, and two put ten thousand to flight, unless their Rock had sold them, and the LORD had given them up?"

Appendix

1. Matthew 25:21, 23: "His master said to him, 'Well done, good and faithful slave. You were faithful with a few things, I will put you in charge of many things; enter into the joy of your master.'"

2. John 15:8: "My Father is glorified by this, that you bear much fruit, and so prove to be My disciples."

3. Corinthians 11:1: "Be imitators of me, just as I also am of Christ."

4. Luke 6:12-13: "It was at this time that He went off to the mountain to pray, and He spent the whole night in prayer to God. And when day came, He called His disciples to Him and chose twelve of them, whom He also named as apostles"

5. Frank Whaling, ed. *John and Charles Wesley* (Mahwah, N.J.: Paulist Press, 1981), 387.

Sources Consulted

Castellanos, Cesar. *Developing a Supernatural Leadership.* Bogota: G12 Editores, 2003.

_____. *The Ladder of Success.* Bogota: Editorial Vilit & Co. Ltd., 2003.

_____. *Successful Leadership Through the Government of 12.* San Jose, Calif.: Spirit-Filled Productions, 2002.

_____. *Transitioning to the Cell Church Philosophy.* Audiotape of lecture presented at the Fourth Convention of Multiplication and Revival, January 1999.

Clark, Jim. *The School of the Vision of the Twelve.* Baton Rouge, La.: Bethany World Prayer Center, 2003.

_____. "The School of the Vision of Twelve." San Diego: G12 Conference, November 4-6, 2004.

Comiskey, Joel. *From 12 to 3.* Houston: Touch Publications, 2002.

_____. *Groups of 12.* Houston: Touch Publications, 1999.

_____. *Home Cell Group Explosion.* Houston: Touch Publications, 1998.

Dye, Colin. "Fulfilling the Mandate." *Harvest Magazine,* Europe Edition, G12 Special Issue. London: Dovewell Communications, 2001.

Fajardo, Cesar. "Every Member a Multitude" Conference. Baton Rouge, La.: International Cell Conference, September 15, 2004.

Hadidian, Allen. *Successful Discipling.* Chicago: Moody Press, 1979.

Malloy, Rocky J. *The Jesus System Groups of 12.* Texas City, Tex.: Impact Productions, 2002.

Manual, Church of the Nazarene. Kansas City: Nazarene Publishing House, 2001.

Porter, Jerry. Board of Trustees Meeting, Nazarene Theological Seminary, Kansas City, May 1, 2004.

Rodriguez, Freddy. *A Successful Cell Vision,* videotape of lecture presented at the Cell Church Conference in Bogota, Colombia, 1996.

Schmelzer, Steve. G12 Lecture, Pastor's Leadership Conference, San Diego, July 28, 2004.

Stockstill, Larry. "Every Member a Multitude" Conference. Baton Rouge, La.: International Cell Conference, September 14, 2004.

_____. *The Cell Church.* Ventura, Calif.: Regal Books, 1998.

Vaughan, John. "K Church" Conference. San Diego, January 23, 2002.

Wilke, Richard B. *And Are We Yet Alive?* Nashville: Abingdon Press, 1986.